handy homework helper

Science

Writer:
Devi Mathieu

Consultant:
Edee Norman Wiziecki

Publications International, Ltd.

Devi Mathieu is a prolific writer and editor specializing in science and education. She is a member of the Northern California Science Writers Association and holds a B.A. in Biology from San Francisco State University.

Edee Norman Wiziecki is K-8 Science Coordinator at Franklin Science Center, Champaign Community Schools Unit District #4. She was named Outstanding Science Teacher of Illinois, 1985-1987, by the National Science Teachers Association and holds a Masters in Education with an emphasis in Science Education from the University of Illinois.

Reference art research: Joyce Stirniman, Creative Services Associates, Inc.

Cover photography: Siede Preis Photography

Models and agencies: McBlaine & Associates, Inc.: Charles Beavers, Kimmie Reed; **Royal Modeling Management:** Bonney Bowman, Jessica Shrader; Sean St.Onge.

Photo credits: Animals Animals: Bill Beatty: 21 (bottom top right); E.R. Degginger: 21 (bottom left); Zig Leszczynski: 24 (left center); Scott W. Smith: 21 (bottom right); D.R. Specker: 21 (bottom top left & bottom top center); Doug Wechsler: 20 (bottom left); Earth Scenes: Bill Beatty: 79 (bottom); G.E. Bernard: 7 (bottom); E.R. Degginger: 54 (center & bottom); John Lemker: 120 (bottom); C.C. Lockwood: 96 (top); Breck P. Kent: 96 (center & bottom left), 97 (bottom right center); Robert Maier: 54 (top); Thane: 100 (top); **Joel E. Arem:** 98 (bottom left & bottom right);

Dr. Charles R. Belinky/©Educational Images Ltd., Elmira, NY. Used by permission: 90 (top); **FPG International:** Charles Benes: 46 (center); Gary Buss: 49 (left center), 50 (bottom); Bruce Byers: 74 (center); Jeri Gleiter: 81 (top left); Rob Goldman: 86 (left); Guy Marché: 100 (bottom); Buddy Mays: 23 (left center); NASA: contents (bottom left), 66 (center); Michael Nelson: 77 (bottom); Stan Osolinski: 122 (left center); Terry Qing: 28 (bottom top center); Howard G. Ross: 102 (right center); Al Satterwhite: 26 (top right); Scott Mark: 66 (bottom); Ulf Sjostedt: 108 (bottom); V.I. LAB E.R.I.C.: 5 (bottom); L. West: 17 (top left); Jack Zehrt: 112 (left); **Bruce Hawkins/Lassen:** 49 (bottom left); **International Stock:** contents (bottom right), 112 (right); Mike Agliolo: 91; Wayne Aldridge: 50 (center); Warren Faidley: 68 (bottom); Chuck Mason: 64 (top); Radie Nedlin: 64 (bottom); Valder/Tormey: 72 (top); **Kraft General Food:** 56 (center); **Dan McCoy/Rainbow:** 76 (bottom left); **Robert & Linda Mitchell:** 97 (top right center & bottom); NASA: 119 (bottom); **JoAnn Ordano/Photo/Nats, Inc.:** 97 (top); **Photri, Inc.:** 7 (top), 11 (top left center), 13 (bottom), 17 (top right), 32 (top), 46 (left), 66 (top), 102 (top), 122 (right center); Lewis H. Ellsworth: 102 (left center); Hungerford: 23 (right center); Lani: 28 (center); Microstock: contents (top right), 6 (bottom); Rob Simpson: 29 (right); **SuperStock:** 5 (top), 11 (bottom left center & bottom), 12 (bottom left & bottom right), 28 (top, top left, bottom & bottom center), 33 (top), 42 (top), 46 (right & bottom), 49 (right center, bottom center & bottom right); 50 (top), 55 (bottom), 56 (bottom), 61 (center & bottom), 63, 74 (top left & right), 75 (top), 79 (top), 81 (top right), 83 (top), 85 (bottom), 90 (bottom), 101 (top), 108 (bottom top left & bottom center), 115 (bottom); David Northcott: 30 (bottom); **Kurt Williams:** 83 (bottom); **Kent Wood:** 56 (top), 76 (top, center & bottom right).

Illustrations: Bob Masheris. Additional illustrations: Thomas Cranmer; Steve Fuller; Brad Gaber; Mike Gardner; Peg Gerrity; Glasgow & Associates Information Graphics; Lorie Robare; Richard Stergulz; Wild Onion Studio.

Contents

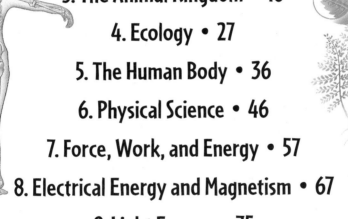

About This Book

Homework takes time and a lot of hard work. Many students would say it's their least favorite part of the school day. But it's also one of the most important parts of your school career because it does so much to help you learn. Learning gives you knowledge, and knowledge gives you power.

Homework gives you a chance to review the material you've been studying so you understand it better. It lets you work on your own, which can give you confidence and independence. Doing school work at home also gives your parents a way to find out what you're studying in school.

Everyone has trouble with their homework from time to time, and *Handy Homework Helper: Science* can help you when you run into a problem. This book was prepared with the help of educational specialists. It offers quick, simple explanations of the basic material that you're studying in school. If you get stuck on an idea or have trouble finding some information, *Handy Homework Helper: Science* can help clear it up for you. It can also help your parents help you by giving them a fast refresher course in the subject.

This book is clearly organized by the topics you'll be studying in Science. A quick look at the Table of Contents will tell you which chapter covers the area you're working on. You can probably guess which chapter includes what you need and then flip through the chapter until you find it. For even more help finding what you're looking for, look up key words related to what you're studying in the Index. You might find material faster that way, and you might also find useful information in a place you wouldn't have thought to look.

Remember that different teachers and different schools take different approaches to teaching Science. For that reason, we recommend that you talk with your teacher about using this homework guide. You might even let your teacher look through the book so he or she can help you use it in a way that best matches what you're studying at school.

Organizing Living Things

Living Things Are Alike in Many Ways

Living things come in an amazing variety of forms. A flower is very different from a giraffe. An earthworm is not much like a bird. But all these are living things with several features in common. These features are the characteristics of life, and they can be used to distinguish living things from nonliving things.

All living things produce young of their own kind.

All living things share the following characteristics:

• All living things need food.

• All living things produce young of their own kind.

• All living things grow and change.

• All living things eliminate wastes.

• All living things respond to the world around them.

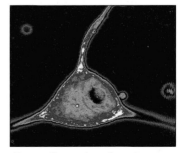

Nerve cell seen through a microscope.

• All living things are made of cells.

Cells Are the Building Blocks of Life

All living organisms are made up of tiny units called **cells**. Cells are so small they can be seen only with the help of a microscope. Different kinds of cells make up different kinds of tissues and structures. These tissues and structures perform specialized tasks. For example, the muscle cells of a hawk enable the bird to move its wings. The cells in a plant's leaf help the plant use sunlight to make the food it needs. Inside every cell are many smaller parts, each with a different job to do:

Animal cell

The **cell membrane** is a flexible covering that surrounds and protects the cell. Substances can pass into and out of the cell through the cell membrane.

The **nucleus** controls the rest of the cell. It sends messages to all other parts of the cell, telling each part what to do.

The **cytoplasm** is a jellylike substance inside the cell. All the other parts of the cell float in the cytoplasm.

Chromosomes are inside the nucleus. They contain all the cell's operating instructions. The chromosomes are made of proteins and a complex material called DNA. DNA directs the cell's activities.

Mitochondria supply the cell with the energy needed to carry on life's processes. Enzymes in the mitochondria break down organic molecules and release the energy contained in them.

The **cell wall** is a rigid structure that surrounds each cell of a plant. The cell wall helps make plants stiff enough to grow upright. It also prevents water loss. Animal cells do not have cell walls.

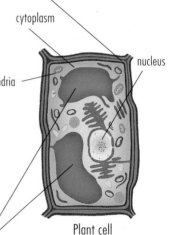

cytoplasm

nucleus

mitochondria

Plant cell

Chloroplasts capture sunlight that plants need for growth. Animal cells do not contain chloroplasts.

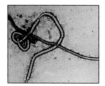

Ebola virus

Viruses are nonliving particles that are simpler than living cells. They contain DNA and can reproduce only by invading the cells of living organisms. Some viruses cause illnesses like the common cold or the measles.

Classifying Organisms

Earth is home to millions of different kinds of living organisms. Scientists separate organisms into five major groups, called **kingdoms**.

Moneran Kingdom

Bacteria

Monerans are commonly known as **bacteria**. They are single-celled organisms that usually grow in groups, or **colonies**. They are found almost everywhere on earth: in air, in soil, inside the bodies of animals, in lakes and streams, even at the bottom of the ocean. Each bacteria cell is surrounded by a cell wall, but its nucleus is not surrounded by a membrane. Most bacteria absorb food from their surroundings, though some can use the energy from sunlight to make food. Some bacteria cause diseases in humans and animals.

Protist Kingdom

Amoeba

The **protist** kingdom includes a wide variety of organisms that live in moist environments. Their cells contain true nuclei and are much more complex than the cells of monerans. Protists include single-celled creatures like *Amoeba*, as well as many-celled organisms like green algae and seaweeds. Some protists capture and eat other organisms. Some use the energy from sunlight to make their own food. Some use both methods to obtain their food.

Fungi Kingdom

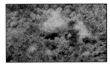

Bread mold

Fungi include mushrooms, molds, and mildew. Most fungi are many-celled organisms that live in shady, moist environments. They feed by breaking down and absorbing nutrients from dead organisms. Fungi cannot make their own food. But, like plants, fungi have cell walls. Bread mold is a fungus, as are the yeasts used to make bread dough rise. Fungus cells are complex and contain true nuclei. *Penicillium* is a fungus. From it we get penicillin, a drug used to fight illnesses caused by members of the moneran kingdom, bacteria.

Plant Kingdom

Plants are many-celled organisms that use energy from sunlight to make their own food. Plant cells are complex, contain true nuclei, and have thick cell walls. Plants reproduce by forming spores or seeds. Plants include ferns, mosses, trees, herbs, and flowering plants. They cover much of the land surface of the earth. Their leaves, stems, seeds, fruits, flowers, and roots are important sources of food and shelter for other organisms, including humans.

Fern

Herb

Flowering plant

Animal Kingdom

Animals are many-celled organisms that feed on other organisms. Once an animal has eaten, it breaks down, or digests, the food. Animal cells are complex. They have true nuclei but do not have cell walls. Animals have muscles and nerves that enable them to move from place to place. Most reproduce by forming a fertilized egg, called a **zygote**, that grows into a new individual. Many different kinds of animals live on earth, including jellyfish, worms, snails, insects, reptiles, amphibians, birds, and mammals such as dogs, elephants, and humans.

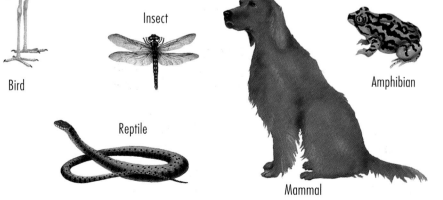

Insect

Bird

Amphibian

Reptile

Mammal

Classifying Organisms into Smaller Groups

Scientists use a special system of classification to break each kingdom down into smaller and smaller units. A kingdom contains several **phyla**, each phylum is made up of **classes**, each class can be separated into smaller **orders**, and so on. The smaller the category, the more similarities its members share.

Every organism that has been observed and studied by humans has a **scientific name**. This name is made up of the organism's **genus** and **species**. Organisms with the same name are members of the same species. A species is a group of organisms that look and act alike and can mate to produce fertile offspring.

House cats and mountain lions are closely related, but they are not the same species. The cat's scientific name is *Felis domestica*. The mountain lion's scientific name is *Felis concolor*.

Kingdom: Animal

Phylum: Chordata

Class: Mammal

Order: Carnivora

Family: Felidae

Genus: *Felis*

Felis domestica

Species: *domestica*

Species: *concolor*

Felis concolor

The Plant Kingdom

Plants are living organisms made up of cells that have thick walls. Green plants use the sun's energy to make food in a process called **photosynthesis**. Photosynthesis takes place in **chloroplasts** inside plant cells. Plants are green because chloroplasts contain a green pigment, called **chlorophyll**, that traps sunlight.

Seedless Plants

Mosses and ferns are plants that reproduce by forming **spores** rather than seeds. A spore is a cell that can grow into a new moss or fern plant. Spores do not contain a food supply for the first few days of the new plant's life. You can compare seedless plants with the seed-producing plants on the following pages.

Mosses live in moist, cool environments. They are usually only a few inches tall and have tiny leaves. They produce spores in capsules at the top of stalks.

Ferns also prefer moist, cool environments, but some can grow in sunny, fairly dry areas. Ferns are larger than mosses and may grow several feet tall. Ferns have underground stems called rhizomes. Roots grow down from the rhizomes. Ferns have long, graceful fronds instead of leaves. Spores are produced on the underside of fronds.

Seed-Producing Plants

Most plants reproduce by making seeds. A seed contains a plant **embryo**, a food supply, and a hard protective covering, or seed coat. An embryo is a tiny, very young plant. Plants that produce seeds are an important food source for humans and other animals.

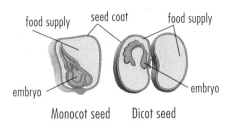

food supply   seed coat   food supply

embryo   embryo

Monocot seed   Dicot seed

Monocot seeds have one seed leaf, or **cotyledon**, in the embryo. Dicot seeds have two.

Each of the woody scales of a pine cone bears a seed at its base.

Cone-Bearing Plants

Cone-bearing plants produce seeds inside cone-shaped structures. These are called pine cones. Trees such as pine, fir, redwood, cedar, and larch are examples of cone-bearing plants. Most have needle-shaped leaves that stay on the tree through the winter.

Flowering Plants

Flowering plants produce seeds inside a fruit. Most of the plants on earth today are flowering plants. Grasses, weeds, daisies, beans, tomatoes, and carrots are all flowering plants. Oak trees and maple trees also belong to this group.

Almond trees produce seeds inside a dry fruit. Other plants produce seeds inside fleshy fruit, such as an apple.

Cone-bearing trees have needles that stay green all winter. Flowering trees have leaves that change colors in the autumn and fall off in the winter.

Roots Anchor and Absorb

All seed-producing plants have **roots.** They help hold the plant in the soil. Roots also absorb water and minerals from the soil. They carry the water and minerals to the stem.

Plants spread their **roots** far through the soil so they are anchored more securely and so they can find more water and nutrients. Tiny, delicate **root hairs** cover the growing ends of the roots. The root hairs absorb water and nutrients from the soil. Once the water and nutrients are absorbed, they move into larger and larger branches of the root. The thick central part of the root, sometimes called the **taproot,** carries the nutrients up into the plant stem.

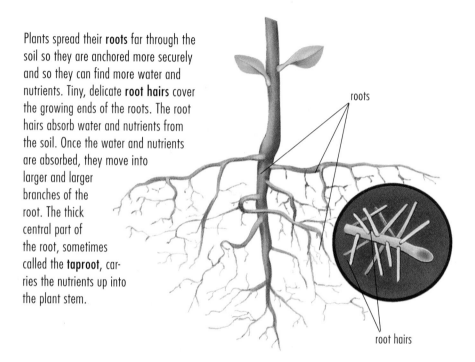

roots

root hairs

Some plants, such as carrots and radishes, store food in their roots. These starch-filled roots provide food for humans and other animals.

Stems Support and Transport

The **stem** of the plant carries water, nutrients, and food to different parts of the plant. It also provides support to help hold the plant upright. Some plants, like celery and rhubarb, store food in their stems.

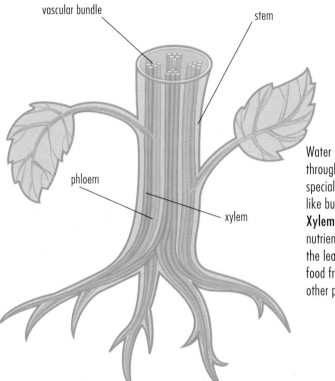

vascular bundle

stem

phloem

xylem

Water and nutrients move through the stem inside special tissues that look like bundles of tiny tubes. **Xylem** carries water and nutrients from the roots to the leaves. **Phloem** carries food from the leaves to the other parts of the plant.

Trees and other plants that live longer than a year develop woody stems. The trunk of a tree is its stem. For every year of a tree's growth, rings of cells are added to the trunk, making it thicker and stronger. The age of a tree can be determined by counting these rings.

Leaves Are Food Factories

Leaves capture sunlight to make food. Water and nutrients move from the stem into the leaves through the **veins** of the leaf. The undersides of leaves have tiny openings called **stomata**. The stomata open and close to allow gases—carbon dioxide, oxygen, and water vapor—to move in and out of the plant.

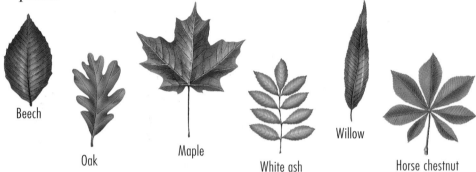

Beech

Oak

Maple

White ash

Willow

Horse chestnut

A leaf is attached to the plant by a stalk called the **petiole**. The shapes of leaves and their vein patterns are used in plant identification.

Transpiration—Moving Water

Water moves through a plant through a process called **transpiration**. When water is heated up it turns into water vapor. When leaves are heated by sunlight, the water in them becomes vapor. It escapes through the open stomata. As leaves lose water in this way, they pull more water up from the roots. The outside of most leaves is covered with a waxy layer, called a **cuticle**. The cuticle helps prevent too much water loss.

waxy cuticle

waxy cuticle

water vapor

stomata

Photosynthesis–
Plants Make Food

Plants produce their own food through the process known as **photosynthesis.** Photosynthesis takes place in green **chloroplasts** inside leaf cells. The chloroplasts absorb energy from sunlight. The roots and stem bring water to the leaves. The stomata allow the gas carbon dioxide to enter the leaves. The chloroplasts use the sun's energy to make food from the water and carbon dioxide. This food is in the form of sugars.

energy from sunlight

carbon dioxide

carbon dioxide

water

water

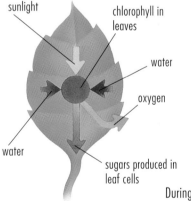

sunlight

chlorophyll in leaves

water

oxygen

water

sugars produced in leaf cells

During photosynthesis, plants release oxygen into the air. Plants help maintain the supply of oxygen that animals need.

Respiration–Releasing Energy

All cells need energy. To grow, plants use the energy contained in the sugars produced through photosynthesis. The plant cells take in oxygen. They use the oxygen to break the sugar down into water and carbon dioxide. This interaction releases energy for the plant cells to use. It also produces carbon dioxide, which the plant releases into the air. The entire process of taking in and releasing gases is called **respiration**.

How Flowering Plants Reproduce

Flowers

Flowers produce the seeds that will become new flowering plants. Each part of the flower has a job to do.

The **pistil** is the female part of the flower. The sticky or feathery area at the top of the pistil is called the **stigma**. The stigma is attached to the ovary by a long tube called the **style**.

The **stamen** is the male part of the flower. Pollen is produced in the **anthers** at the top of the stamen.

Perfume or sweet nectar in **nectaries** at the base of petals helps attract pollinators.

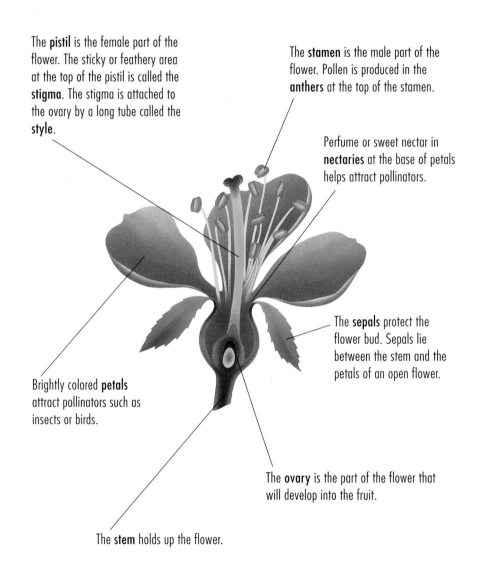

The **sepals** protect the flower bud. Sepals lie between the stem and the petals of an open flower.

Brightly colored **petals** attract pollinators such as insects or birds.

The **ovary** is the part of the flower that will develop into the fruit.

The **stem** holds up the flower.

Pollinators and Pollination

Bees, butterflies, other insects, hummingbirds, and even bats help flowers reproduce. These animals carry **pollen** from one flower to another. When a pollinator visits a flower to sip nectar, pollen sticks to the pollinator's body. When the pollinator visits another flower, some of the pollen rubs off onto the stigma. This process is called **pollination**.

Seeds

The pollen grains travel down the style and into the ovary. The pollen grains fertilize the egg cells in the ovules, and seeds begin to form. As the seeds develop, the walls of the ovary grow into the fruit that will contain the seeds.

The Animal Kingdom

Invertebrates

Most species in the animal kingdom do not have backbones. Animals without backbones are called **invertebrates**. Invertebrates are divided into many groups. Each group has distinct features.

Sponges (Poriferans)

Sponges are the simplest of all the animals. All sponges live in water, and most are found in the ocean. The body of a sponge has many openings through which water moves. Sponges cannot move from place to place to find food. They strain ocean water through their bodies to trap tiny food particles.

Sponge

Animals with Stinging Cells (Cnidarians)

These invertebrates have tentacles covered with stinging cells. They use their tentacles to capture food. Jellyfish float on the surface of the ocean and capture fish and other swimming animals. Sea anemones live on the ocean bottom, attached to rocks. They hold their tentacles out into the water to capture animals that swim by. Corals are like sea anemones, except that their bodies have a hard covering. Corals grow together in colonies that form coral reefs.

Sea anemone

Spiny Skinned Animals (Echinoderms)

These animals have hard, spiny skin and are found only in the ocean. Starfish, or sea stars, crawl slowly over the ocean floor, looking for animals to eat. Sea urchins are covered with spines that are often long and very sharp. Sand dollars are sea urchins with short, soft spines. Sand dollars burrow into the sand in shallow ocean waters.

Starfish

Worms

Worms are long, soft-bodied animals. **Flatworms** are small and have a thin, flattened body. Some flatworms live in lakes, ponds, or ocean waters. Others live inside the bodies of animals. **Roundworms** are small, cylinder-shaped worms that

live in soil, water, or the bodies of plants or animals. Earthworms and leeches are **segmented worms.** These worms have ring-like sections, or segments. Other kinds of segmented worms live in freshwater and in the ocean.

Earthworm

Mollusks

Mollusks are soft-bodied animals that usually have shells. Snails and slugs live on moist land or in water. Snails have shells. Slugs do not. Snails and slugs glide slowly along the ground or ocean bottom searching for plants or

Snail

algae to eat. Clams, oysters, mussels, and scallops live in water. They have two shells that open and close. Clams burrow in sand or mud at the bottom of oceans, lakes, and rivers. Oysters and mussels attach themselves to ocean rocks. Scallops propel themselves through the water

Mussels

by rapidly opening and closing their shells. Octopuses and squid have no shells. They use their long tentacles to capture animals to eat.

Squid

Octopus

Arthropods

Arthropods make up the largest phylum in the animal kingdom. Every arthropod has jointed legs and a skeleton that covers the outside of its body. This is called an **exoskeleton**. As it grows, an arthropod sheds its skeleton to grow a new, larger one. Some arthropods have antennae, claws, and pincers.

Crustaceans have ten legs, at least one pair of antennae, and jaws for crushing food. Most crustaceans, including crabs, shrimp, lobsters, crayfish, and barnacles, live in water. A few, such as pillbugs, live on moist land.

Crab

Arachnids have eight legs, two body segments, and no antennae. This group includes spiders, scorpions, mites, and ticks.

Centipedes and **millipedes** look like segmented worms with legs. They live in damp land environments. Centipedes have one pair of legs for each segment. Millipedes have two pairs of legs for each segment.

Spider

Millipede

Insects

Insects are arthropods with six legs and three body regions: **head, thorax,** and **abdomen.** Most insects have one or two pairs of wings, though some have no wings at all.

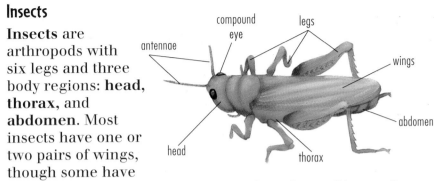

Bees, beetles, ants, flies, butterflies, and mosquitoes are insects you have probably seen.

The body form of many insects changes as they develop from egg to adult. This change is called **metamorphosis.** Butterflies, bees, flies, and beetles go through **complete metamorphosis.** Aphids, crickets, and grasshoppers go through **simple metamorphosis.** Scientists also call simple metamorphosis **incomplete metamorphosis.**

Complete metamorphosis of a butterfly

Egg

Larva

Caterpillar

Cocoon containing pupa

Adult

Vertebrates

Vertebrates are animals with backbones. Most vertebrates have a skeleton made of bone inside their bodies. Fish, reptiles, and amphibians are **cold-blooded** vertebrates. Their body temperature changes with the temperature of their surroundings. Birds and mammals are warm-blooded vertebrates. The body temperature of **warm-blooded** animals stays about the same no matter how hot or cold the surroundings are.

Fish

Fish live in water. They have **fins** and **gills**, and their skin is usually covered with **scales**. Fish use their fins to move through the water. Gills are used for breathing. As water passes over the gills, they absorb oxygen and release carbon dioxide. Scales are hard, thin plates that cover and help protect the body of the fish.

Thousands of species of fish exist. They live in almost every body of water on earth. **Freshwater fish** live in lakes and streams. Catfish stay near the bottom and use their long, sensitive whiskers to help find food. Trout are strong swimmers that catch insects and smaller fish to eat. **Saltwater fish** come in an amazing variety of forms. Sharks and rays have skeletons made of flexible cartilage instead of bone. Humans' ears and noses are made of cartilage. Brightly colored angelfish live in warm, tropical oceans. Eels live in rocky crevices. Seahorses are fish that live among fronds of algae.

Trout

Seahorse

Angelfish

Eel

Amphibians

Amphibians have moist, smooth skin without scales. Young amphibians have gills and live in water. Adult amphibians have lungs and live on land or in water. Amphibians can also breathe through their very thin skin. Amphibians have two pairs of legs.

Frogs lay their eggs in water. The eggs hatch into young **tadpoles** that live in the water. Tadpoles have tails and gills. They eat plants. They gradually develop legs and lungs and lose their tails and gills. Adult frogs are at home in water and on land. They use their long, sticky tongues to catch insects and other animals.

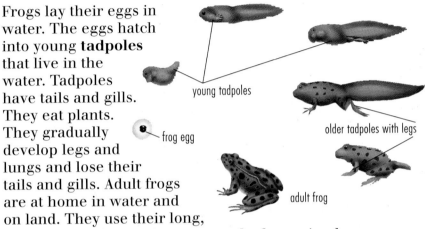

young tadpoles

frog egg

older tadpoles with legs

adult frog

It's usually easy to tell frogs and toads apart. Most frogs *(left)* have smooth, shiny skin. Most toads *(right)* have dry, rough, warty-looking skin.

Adult salamanders live on land in moist, shady areas. They stay under cover during the day. At night, salamanders hunt for worms and insects to eat.

Reptiles

Reptiles have thick, dry skin covered with scales. Almost all reptiles except snakes have four legs and claws. The claws are used for walking, digging, and climbing. Reptiles have lungs for breathing and lay eggs on the ground. Reptile eggs are covered with thick, leathery shells.

Today's reptiles are descended from the same ancestors as the dinosaurs. Dinosaurs are now extinct. They lived hundreds of millions of years ago.

A turtle can draw its head and legs into its shell for protection. Turtles that live in water must come to the surface to breathe air through their lungs. Most turtles eat plants, but snapping turtles catch and eat fish, amphibians, and swimming birds.

Snakes are legless reptiles found all over the world. They shed their skin from time to time as they grow. Snakes eat insects, eggs, fish, mice and other rodents, and amphibians.

Lizards live in all but the coldest regions of earth. Many live in very hot, dry climates. Lizards may be found living in underground burrows, on the ground, in trees, and even in water. Most lizards eat insects. Some eat plants, and a few lizards catch and eat other animals.

Birds

Birds are the only animals with feathers. They have one pair of wings and one pair of legs covered with scales. The legs end in claws used for perching and sometimes for capturing food. Birds lay eggs that have a hard, protective shell. Parent birds keep their eggs warm until they hatch. The parents bring food to the young until they are old enough to fly.

Seed-eating birds, such as the finch, have strong beaks that can crack hard seed coats. The flycatcher and other insect-eating birds have longer, more delicate beaks. The hummingbird uses its long beak and tongue to suck nectar from deep inside flowers.

Birds have two kinds of feathers. Long, straight **contour feathers** are used for flight. They are found on the bird's wings, body, and tail. Fluffy **down feathers** lie between the contour feathers and the body. These soft feathers help birds stay warm.

Owls, hawks, and eagles are birds of prey. They feed on rodents, snakes, and smaller birds. They have keen vision that enables them to see prey from high in the sky.

All birds have wings, but some birds cannot fly. Penguins use their wings for swimming underwater. Ostriches have well-developed legs for running along the ground.

Mammals

Mammals are the only animals with hair or fur. Mammals also have highly developed brains that help them learn and remember.

All mammals nurse their young. Mammal parents protect and care for their young until they are able to care for themselves.

A mother mammal nursing her young.

Zebra

Mammals are found almost everywhere on earth. Whales and dolphins live in the ocean. Giraffes, elephants, and zebras live in the grasslands of Africa. Polar bears live on frozen Arctic ice. Moles live in underground burrows.

Bats are the only mammals capable of true flight. Their front legs have developed into leathery wings. They live in caves or hollow trees and are active at night.

Humans, gorillas, and chimpanzees all belong to the group of mammals called **primates**. Primates have hands that can grasp objects.

Kangaroos and opossums are **marsupials**, mammals that carry their young in a body pouch. Marsupials are found mainly in Australia, but the opossum lives in North America.

Cetaceans such as whales and dolphins are mammals that live their whole lives in the water.

Ecology

The Biosphere

The **biosphere** is the region of the earth where life is found. The biosphere stretches from the deepest oceans to the highest parts of the atmosphere. The smallest parts of the biosphere are the individual **organisms** living in it. **Ecology** is the study of how the organisms of earth's biosphere interact with each other and with their environment.

Ecosystems

An **ecosystem** is made up of the living parts plus the nonliving parts of the environment. The nonliving, or **abiotic**, part includes water, sunlight, temperature, and weather. The living organisms in the ecosystem are called the **biotic** part. The grassland ecosystem shown below includes the organisms of the grassland community, plus the dirt, rocks, air, sunlight, and rain. Organisms depend on the nonliving parts of their ecosystem for survival.

Biomes

Biomes are ecosystems that have similar characteristics. All the biomes on earth make up the biosphere.

 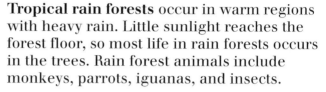

Tropical rain forests occur in warm regions with heavy rain. Little sunlight reaches the forest floor, so most life in rain forests occurs in the trees. Rain forest animals include monkeys, parrots, iguanas, and insects.

Forests receive enough rainfall to support the growth of tall trees. **Evergreen forests** are composed of pine, fir, redwood, and other evergreen trees. **Deciduous forests** have maple, oak, elm, and other trees that lose their leaves every winter. Forest animals include birds, skunks, wolves, and snakes.

Grasslands are covered with small plants that can survive hot, dry weather. Animals of the grasslands include buffalo and prairie dogs in North America, gazelles and zebras in Africa, and kangaroos in Australia.

Deserts have poor soil and receive little rain. The desert is usually covered with bare soil, cacti, and a few hardy shrubs and trees. Desert animals include snakes, scorpions, coyotes, and roadrunners.

Saltwater ecosystems include coral reefs, rocky tidepools, deep sea canyons, and other ocean environments. Whales, seals, fish, algae, and plankton live in the world's oceans.

Freshwater ecosystems include lakes, ponds, rivers, and streams. They occur all over the world in almost every climate. They are home to water plants, fish, turtles, beavers, and many other organisms.

Populations

A **population** is all the organisms of one species living in the same place at the same time. Bullfrogs in a pond are a population. Pond lilies growing in the pond are another population.

Communities

Populations that live together and influence one another are called **communities**. A pond community includes frogs, dragonflies, pond lilies, and birds. Frogs rest on pond lilies. Frogs and birds eat dragonflies, and some birds eat frogs.

Populations Are Always Changing

The size of a population is measured by counting the number of individuals in it. If there is plenty of food and living space, the population can grow. If food is scarce or conditions become too crowded, the population shrinks.

Over time, populations tend to grow in size. A population will stop growing when it reaches the limits of its food supply and living space.

Predators and Prey

Predator

Predators are animals that hunt other animals for food. The hunted animals are called **prey**. Foxes are predators that prey on mice and other small animals. When the mouse population is large, there is plenty of food for foxes, and the fox population

Prey

can grow. But a large population of foxes might eat most of the mice. If that happens, there are fewer mice for the foxes to eat. If the foxes do not find another source of food, their population will stop growing and might even shrink.

Extinction–When Populations Disappear

Sometimes populations shrink in size until there are no more individuals left. If all the populations of a species disappear, that species becomes **extinct**. An extinct species is lost forever.

Dinosaurs became extinct millions of years ago.

Some of the plants and animals living on earth today are **endangered species**. They are in danger of becoming extinct because their populations have become very small. Examples of endangered species include the black rhinoceros of Africa, the Siberian tiger, the American crocodile, and the African elephant.

American crocodile

Extinction can occur for many reasons. A species can become extinct if it is overhunted by predators. For example, millions of passenger pigeons once nested in North American forests, but they were hunted to extinction by humans early in the 20th century.

Species can also become extinct because of changes in their habitat. Grizzly bears and Siberian tigers are threatened with extinction because they need a large territory in which to hunt for food. As the human population grows, the hunting lands available to these species become smaller and smaller.

Grizzly bear

Habitat Is Home

The place where an organism lives and where you expect to find it is called its **habitat**. The habitat of a fox is the burrow it digs under the roots of a tree. The habitat of a humpback whale is the open ocean. Bats roost on the ceilings of caves, blue jays live in trees, and millipedes live in the soil. Those are their habitats.

Niche Is Livelihood

In addition to a habitat, every species has a **niche**. A niche is the way a species lives. A species' niche includes the foods it eats, the way it finds food, the way it searches for and builds its home, and the way it moves through its environment.

Picture a blue jay perched on a tree branch eating an insect. The tree is the blue jay's habitat. The role the blue jay plays in its community is its niche. The jay eats insects. By doing so, it reduces the number of insects that can harm the tree. Blue jays also eat seeds and fruit and discourage other birds from nesting nearby.

Different species can share habitats, but not niches. The leaf litter that covers the forest floor provides a habitat for mushrooms, sow bugs, millipedes, earthworms, and many other organisms. But each of these species has a different niche. The earthworm burrows just beneath the leaf litter. It mixes nutrients from the decaying leaves into the soil. The millipede eats decaying leaves and other dead plant material. Sow bugs burrow into the dead trees for food and protection.

Energy and Living Things

All organisms need energy to live. The sun is the energy source for all life on earth.

Producers Are Food Makers

Producers are organisms that change sunlight into food during photosynthesis. All other living organisms depend on producers for food.

Producers make their own food. Green plants, algae, and single-celled organisms that contain chloroplasts are all producers.

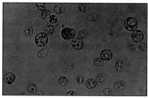
Algae are producers.

Consumers Are Food Takers

Consumers cannot make their own food. They get their energy by eating other organisms. Animals are consumers.

Types of Consumers

Herbivores are consumers that eat only plants.

Rabbits are herbivores.

Carnivores are consumers that eat only animals.

Hawks are carnivores.

Omnivores are consumers that eat both plants and animals.

Raccoons are omnivores.

Predators are carnivores that hunt and kill other animals for food.

Prey are the animals hunted by predators.

Scavengers are carnivores that feed on the bodies of dead animals.

Decomposers Are Food Breakers

Decomposers are nature's recyclers. Decomposers get energy by breaking down, or decomposing, the bodies

Decomposers include microscopic organisms, such as bacteria. Earthworms and fungi are also decomposers.

of dead plants and animals. Decomposition recycles nutrients back into the soil so they can be used for the growth of other organisms.

Food Chains

A **food chain** is a way of describing how organisms depend on one another for food. A food chain also shows how energy from the sun moves from one organism to another.

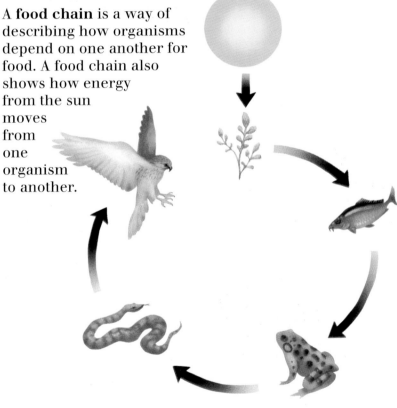

In this food chain, a plant is the producer. A fish eats the plant, a frog eats the fish, a snake eats the frog, and a hawk eats the snake. When the hawk dies, decomposers will break down its body so the nutrients contained in it can be used by other organisms. The plant captures energy from the sun and converts it to food energy. Then each animal gets energy from the organism it eats.

Food Webs

Most ecosystems include many different kinds of producers. And most animals eat more than one kind of food. **Food webs** are networks of food chains that show all the possible feeding relationships in a community.

The food web shown below describes a grassland community in North America. Mice burrow underground, coming up to feed on grass seeds and other plants. Insects, rabbits, and ground squirrels also eat the plants. Rattlesnakes, coyotes, and hawks prey on squirrels and mice. Meadowlarks and frogs feed on insects. When plants and animals die, their bodies are decomposed by fungi, bacteria, and other microscopic organisms.

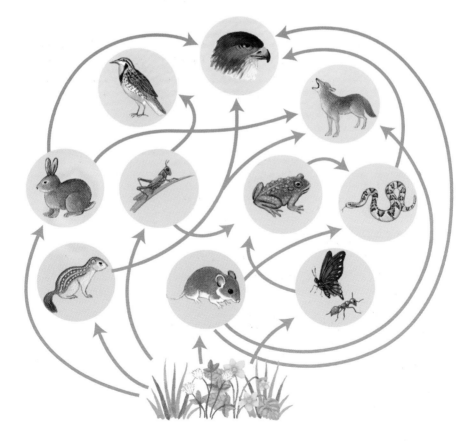

Energy Pyramid

Every organism, from microscopic bacteria to giant whales, needs energy to survive. Producers make their energy from sunlight and water. Consumers get their energy from the organisms they eat. Each step in a food chain or food web actually shows energy moving through the ecosystem. The amount of energy available at each step can be shown by using an **energy pyramid**.

The largest amount of energy is present in the producers of an ecosystem. Some of this energy is used by the producers for their own growth, and some is lost to the atmosphere as heat. Less energy is present at the second level, the herbivores. Here, too, some of the energy is used for growth and some is lost to heat. Less and less energy is available as you move up the pyramid.

Food chains and food webs usually have three or four steps, but never more than five. There is not enough energy left for a sixth level. Carnivores at the top of the energy pyramid are called **top carnivores**. Top carnivores have no predators.

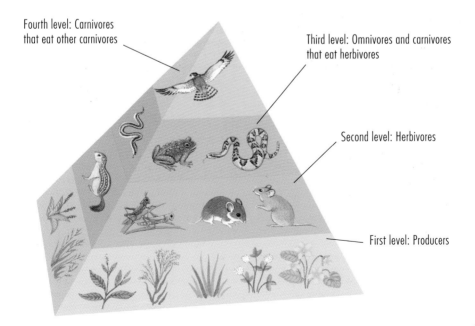

Fourth level: Carnivores that eat other carnivores

Third level: Omnivores and carnivores that eat herbivores

Second level: Herbivores

First level: Producers

The Human Body

The Body's Framework

Bones and Skeletons–Support and Movement

The human skeleton is made up of more than 200 bones. It supports the soft tissues of the body and helps protect delicate internal organs. For example, the skull protects the brain, and the ribs protect the lungs and heart. **Cartilage** is a tough, rubbery material. In some places, it connects bones together. Where bones meet other bones, cartilage covers and protects their ends.

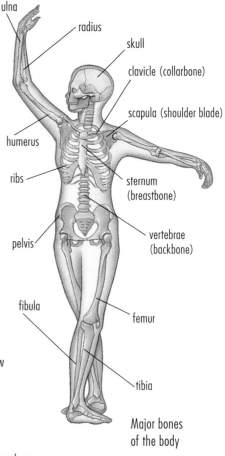

Major bones of the body

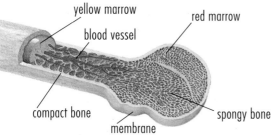

Structure of a bone

A thin, soft **membrane** covers the outside of the bone. Blood vessels in the membrane supply blood to the tissues inside the bone. Calcium and phosphorous in the **compact bone** give the bone its hardness and strength. Compact bone also contains **blood vessels**, bone cells, and nerves. **Spongy bone** is full of tiny holes, like a sponge. It is hard like compact bone, because it also contains calcium and phosphorous. **Yellow marrow** inside the long part of the bone stores fat and makes some white blood cells. **Red marrow** in the spaces in spongy bone creates new blood cells for the body.

Joints and Ligaments–Holding Bones Together

Bones are hard and rigid. They do not bend easily. The human body can bend and move because bones are held together by bendable, movable **joints**. A joint is a place in the body where bones join together. **Ligaments** are tough, flexible tissues that hold the joints together. The human body has several kinds of joints that allow different kinds of movement.

Elbows, knees, fingers, and toes are **hinged joints** that move back and forth, like a door opening and closing on its hinges. Twisting motions of the neck and forearms are controlled by **pivot joints.** Pivot joints allow bones to rotate from side to side. **Ball-and-socket joints** such as shoulders and hips can rotate in many directions. They are formed by the ball-shaped end of one bone fitting into the hollow socket of a neighboring bone. **Gliding joints** allow neighboring bones to glide over one another. The backbone is made up of a series of small bones called vertebrae. Cartilage between each of the vertebrae allows them to slide over each other. There are also gliding joints between many of the small bones in the wrists. The places where the bones of the skull come together do not move at all. **Fixed joints** prevent motion.

Hinged joint and
Pivot joint (Elbow)

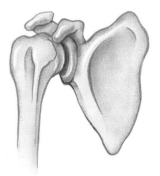

Ball-and-socket joint (Shoulder)

vertebrae cartilage

Gliding joints (Backbone)

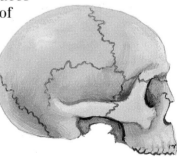

Fixed joints (Skull)

Muscles and Movement

Muscles provide the power needed to move the body. Muscles are made of long cells called **fibers**. Muscle fibers are bundled together.

Muscle fibers can change their shape. When they contract, they become shorter. When they relax, they become longer. Muscles also work in pairs. For example, the two muscles in the upper arm, the triceps and biceps, work together to bend and straighten the arm.

relaxed triceps

contracted biceps

Tendons are bands of stretchy, elastic tissue that connect muscles to bone.

contracted triceps

relaxed biceps

Major muscles of the body

Muscles need energy to do their job. They get energy from a sugar called **glucose**. Blood travels through the entire body and brings glucose and oxygen to all the muscles. Muscle cells use the oxygen to produce energy they need from the glucose. That is why your heart pumps faster and you breathe more rapidly when you exercise. Your blood must circulate faster to carry more oxygen and glucose to your working muscles. Regular exercise makes muscle fibers larger. The larger the fibers, the stronger the muscle.

Types of Muscles

The body has several kinds of muscles. **Voluntary muscles** are those you can control. You decide when to use them to move your arms, legs, neck, and so on. **Involuntary muscles** do their job without your control. Your heart, the muscles used for breathing, and the muscles that move food through your digestive system are involuntary muscles.

Skeletal Muscles

Arm and shoulder muscles

Skeletal muscles are voluntary muscles. They move the bones and joints in the arms, legs, back, neck, and torso.

Cardiac Muscle

Cardiac muscle is involuntary muscle. The heart is made of cardiac muscle. This muscle rhythmically contracts and relaxes to pump blood through the body.

Heart

Smooth Muscle

Smooth muscle is also involuntary muscle. Smooth muscles line the important organs of the body. When smooth muscles contract, they produce a squeezing action. This squeezing helps move food through the stomach and intestines. It also helps move blood through the veins and arteries. Smooth muscles contract more slowly than skeletal muscles do, so they use less energy. This allows them to work longer before they have to rest.

Stomach

Food and Digestion

Digestion is the process of breaking down particles of food into smaller, simpler molecules. The body's cells use these molecules as fuel to produce energy for the body and as raw materials to repair the body and perform other important tasks. The human digestive system includes the mouth, salivary glands, esophagus, stomach, liver, gallbladder, pancreas, small intestine, and large intestine.

The Mouth–Teeth and Saliva

Digestion begins in the mouth. Food is broken off and chewed into smaller pieces by the teeth. The tongue helps position the food so that the teeth can cut and crush it. Chewing is called **mechanical digestion** because the teeth use physical action to break apart the food.

Saliva is a fluid produced by the **salivary glands** and mixed into food during chewing. It is made up of enzymes and an alkaline liquid. The liquid and enzymes chemically break down food. Saliva continues its work as the food travels down to the stomach. The addition of saliva is the first step in the **chemical digestion** of food.

The Esophagus–Moving to the Stomach

Once food has been chewed, the tongue moves it to the back of the mouth. There, it is swallowed. The food passes into the **esophagus**, a muscular tube that joins the mouth to the stomach. As the smooth muscles of the esophagus contract and relax, the food is pushed into the stomach. This muscle action is called **peristalsis**. It is a form of mechanical digestion because it helps crush and grind the food.

The Stomach–Chemical and Mechanical Digestion Continue

The muscles of the **stomach** churn and mix the food. Acids and enzymes from the stomach lining chemically break down the food. In about four hours, a meal of solid food turns into a watery liquid.

The Small Intestine–Digestion Is Completed

Partially digested food passes from the stomach to the **small intestine**. There, it is mixed with digestive fluids produced by the liver and pancreas. The small intestine is narrow and very long. It is coiled to fit inside the body. Smooth muscles contract to move food through it. The food is gradually broken down into molecules small enough to pass through the walls of the intestine and into the bloodstream.

The **liver** is a large, complex organ involved in many of the body's processes. The liver is important in digestion. It produces **bile**. Bile is a chemical that helps break globules of fat into smaller particles. It also helps neutralize stomach acids. Bile is stored in the **gallbladder**.

The **pancreas** produces enzymes that break down all the components of food—carbohydrates, proteins, and fats. Juices produced by the pancreas also help neutralize stomach acids.

The Large Intestine

Material that cannot be digested passes from the small intestine into the **large intestine**. In the large intestine, smooth muscles contract to move this waste along. The walls of the intestine absorb any remaining liquid and pass it into the bloodstream. Only solid waste that cannot be digested is left. This waste leaves the body through the rectum.

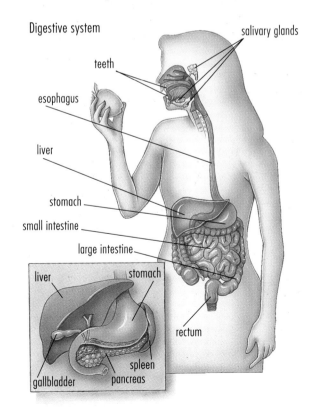

Digestive system

salivary glands

teeth

esophagus

liver

stomach

small intestine

large intestine

liver

stomach

rectum

gallbladder

spleen

pancreas

Blood and Circulation—Carrying Oxygen to the Cells

Blood

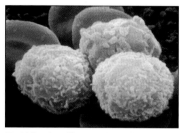

Red bloods cells and white blood cells

Blood is a fluid pumped through the body by the heart. Blood supplies all body cells with oxygen and nutrients. The cells use oxygen to release the energy contained in the nutrients. Blood also carries waste products away from the cells. Waste products can be carbon dioxide, salts, or excess water.

Blood is made up of **red blood cells, white blood cells, platelets,** and **plasma.**

Red blood cells transport oxygen. They get their color from a substance inside them called **hemoglobin.** Hemoglobin carries oxygen. It turns red when it is holding oxygen. White blood cells help fight infection. They destroy bacteria and viruses that invade the body. Platelets help heal wounds. Plasma is the fluid part of the blood. Plasma carries blood cells and platelets, digested food, and water through the circulatory system.

This illustration shows the major veins on the left side of the body in blue and the major arteries on the right side of the body in red.

The Circulatory System

Blood moves through the body in blood vessels. **Arteries** are blood vessels that move oxygen-rich blood from the heart to the rest of the body. The heart pumps blood through the arteries at high pressure. The arteries' walls are thick in order to withstand this pressure. **Veins** carry oxygen-poor blood back to the heart. The blood in the veins flows under less pressure. Veins have valves that keep the blood flowing in one direction.

Capillaries

Capillaries are very tiny blood vessels that lie between arteries and veins. Every cell in the body is near a capillary. As blood travels through the capillaries, nutrients and oxygen move from the blood into the body cells. At the same time, carbon dioxide and other wastes move from the body cells into the blood.

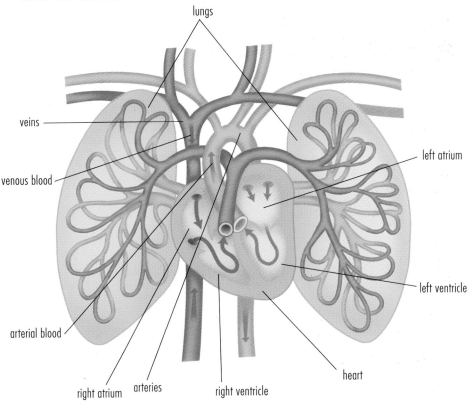

The Heart-Lung System

Blood returning to the heart through the veins has given up its oxygen to the body cells. This blood enters the right side of the heart and is pumped to the lungs. As it moves through the capillaries in the lungs, it absorbs oxygen and releases carbon dioxide. Then it travels to the right side of the heart. From there, the oxygen-rich blood is pumped throughout the body.

Breathing and Respiration–Exchanging Gases

The Respiratory System

Respiration is the process of getting oxygen to the body's cells and removing carbon dioxide from them. Oxygen enters the lungs when air is breathed in, or **inhaled**. Carbon dioxide is released from the lungs when air is breathed out, or **exhaled**.

Air enters the body through the nostrils or the mouth. The air moves through the **pharynx (throat)** to the **larynx (voice box)**. At the top of the larynx is a small flap of tissue called the **epiglottis**. The epiglottis can open and close like a door. When you breathe, it opens to let air into the lungs. When you eat, it closes to keep foods and liquids from entering the lungs.

Air moves through the larynx and **trachea (windpipe)** into the **bronchial tubes** of the lungs. The bronchial tubes get smaller and smaller until they end in tiny sacs called **alveoli**, which are surrounded by capillaries. Carbon dioxide moves from the blood into the alveoli. Oxygen moves from the alveoli into the blood. This process is called **gas exchange**.

The **diaphragm** is a sheetlike muscle that lies beneath the lungs. When the diaphragm contracts, it moves down. Air is pulled into the lungs. When the diaphragm relaxes, it moves up, and air is pushed out of the lungs.

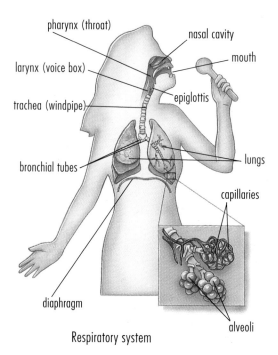

pharynx (throat)

nasal cavity

mouth

larynx (voice box)

epiglottis

trachea (windpipe)

bronchial tubes

lungs

capillaries

diaphragm

alveoli

Respiratory system

Excretion—Getting Rid of Wastes

As cells carry on the processes of life, they produce waste materials that must be removed, or **excreted**, from the body. These waste products include carbon dioxide gas, excess water, salts, and other wastes. As blood moves through capillaries, it collects the wastes from body cells. Carbon dioxide is released from the blood when it reaches the lungs. Other wastes are filtered out of the blood by the **kidneys**.

The kidneys are two fist-sized, bean-shaped organs located in the lower back. Wastes that are filtered from the blood by the kidneys are carried to the bladder. There, they are stored until they are released in the urine.

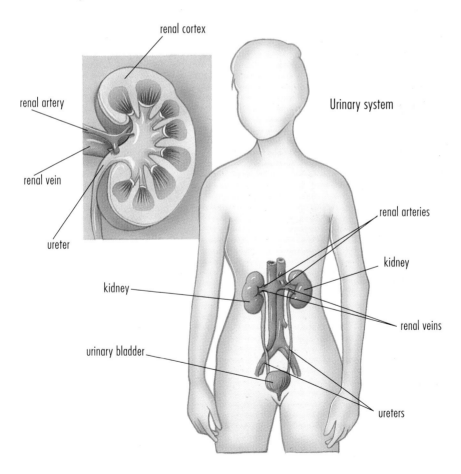

renal cortex

renal artery

renal vein

ureter

Urinary system

renal arteries

kidney

renal veins

kidney

urinary bladder

ureters

Physical Science

Matter

Matter is anything that has mass and takes up space. Every-thing you see and touch is made of matter. Trees, animals, buildings, and cars are made of matter. So are the sun, moon, planets, and stars.

These—and all other—familiar, everyday objects are made up of matter.

Mass

All matter has **mass**. Mass is the amount of matter in an object. The mass of an object does not change unless the amount of matter in it changes.

Mass is not quite the same as **weight**. Weight describes how much the force of gravity pulls on an object. The more massive the object, the more pull gravity has on it. So, the more massive the object, the more it weighs. On earth, the mass of an object is the same as its weight. If you place an object on the moon, its mass will be the same as on earth. But its weight will be one-sixth as much because the moon's gravity is weaker than earth's.

The metric units used to measure weight are the gram (g) and kilo-gram (kg). A nickel weighs about five grams. Two hundred nickels weigh about one kilogram.

Volume

All matter has **volume**. Volume is the space taken up by mat-ter. The metric units used to measure volume are the cubic centimeter (cm³ or cc), the liter (l), and the milliliter (ml). One cubic centimeter is equal to one milliliter.

Density

Density shows how the mass and volume of an object are related. Density is the mass of a substance in a certain unit of volume. We can define density with an equation:

$$\text{Density} = \text{mass/volume}$$

These two gold bars have the same density. They have the same mass. The mass of each bar takes up the same amount of space—it has the same volume.

These two bars have the same volume. But the gold bar has more mass. Because the gold bar packs more mass into the same volume, it has a greater density. Gold has a greater density than chocolate.

The metric units most often used to express density are grams per cubic centimeter (g/cm^3). That tells you how many grams of a substance take up one cubic centimeter of volume. The density of liquid water is $1g/cm^3$. That means an amount of water with one gram of mass takes up one cubic centimeter. The density of gold is $19.3g/cm^3$.

Metric Units Used to Measure Mass, Volume, and Density

MASS

1 kilogram (kg) = 1,000 grams (g)

1 g = 1,000 milligrams (mg)

VOLUME

1 liter (l) = 1,000 milliliters (ml)

1 liter (l) = 1,000 cubic centimeters (cm³ or cc)

DENSITY

mass per unit of volume, or mass/volume

$$\frac{g}{l} \qquad \frac{g}{ml} \qquad \frac{mg}{ml} \qquad \frac{g}{cm^3}$$

The Four Phases of Matter

Matter has four forms: solid, liquid, gas, and plasma. Matter changes from one form to another with changes in temperature and pressure.

Solids have a fixed shape and a fixed volume. Wood, stones, coins, and paper are solids. When water is frozen, it becomes a solid called ice. The particles of matter that make up a solid are tightly packed together.

This scene shows examples of all four states of matter. Can you find them?

They make up a shape that does not change easily.

Liquids flow. A liquid has a fixed volume, but its shape changes to match the shape of its container. Water is a liquid. So are milk, apple juice, and vinegar. The particles of matter that make up a liquid are less tightly packed than the particles of a solid. They are free to move around each other.

Gases are usually invisible. A gas does not have a fixed shape or a fixed volume. A gas will expand to completely fill its container, no matter how large the container is or what shape the container has. Air is a gas. So is the helium used to fill balloons. When water is boiled it becomes a gas called steam, or water vapor. The particles of matter that make up a gas are not packed together at all. Gas particles are free to move in all directions. They tend to spread away from each other.

Plasma is similar to a gas, but its particles are electrically charged. Gases do not have electrically charged particles. Plasma particles exist only at the extremely high temperatures found in the sun.

Properties of Matter

Physical Properties

The **physical properties** of matter describe what you see, feel, and smell when you examine an object. Physical properties include color, odor, shape, and texture. Physical properties also include the phases of matter—solid, liquid, gas, and plasma.

Mass, weight, volume, and density (see pages 46–47) are physical properties of matter. They are also sometimes called general properties of matter.

Physical Changes

When a substance goes through a physical change, its appearance changes but the matter it is made of does not change. Wood that has been carved and polished has gone through a physical change. The appearance of

The wood in this violin has undergone physical changes, but it is still wood, just like this tree stump.

the wood is different, but it is still made up of the same particles of matter. Ice is water that has been physically changed.

Water can be a clear liquid. It can also be solid ice when frozen or gaseous vapor when heated. Whatever form it comes in, though, it's still water.

Iron combines with oxygen to form a new substance with new properties—rust.

Chemical Properties

The **chemical properties** of matter describe what particles make up a substance. If the chemical properties of a substance change, it becomes a completely different substance. For example, if iron is left outdoors, it combines with oxygen to form rust.

Chemical Changes

When a substance goes through a chemical change, there is a change in both its appearance and the matter it is made of. A chemical change results in a new substance with new physical and chemical properties. The burning of wood and the rusting of metal are chemical changes. Chemical changes are also called **chemical reactions**.

Flammability is a chemical property of wood. When wood burns, it changes into new substances—ash and smoke—that have different chemical properties than the wood had.

Sodas and other carbonated drinks contain carbonic acid. As soon as you take the top off the bottle, the carbonic acid goes through a chemical change. It changes into carbon dioxide gas and liquid water. The carbon dioxide gas floats to the surface in the form of bubbles. So the fizz in your favorite soda comes from a chemical change!

The Composition of Matter

All matter is composed of particles that are much too small to see, even with the help of a microscope. We use a model—the atomic model—to help us understand what the particles of matter look like and how they work. A model is a picture, an object, or a mental image that represents something too large, too small, or too complex to study directly.

The Atom

Atoms are the building blocks of matter. Matter is made of many different kinds of atoms. An atom is made of smaller particles called **protons, neutrons,** and **electrons**.

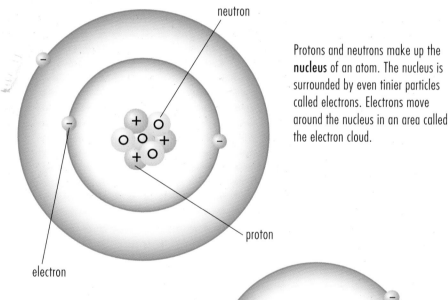

Protons and neutrons make up the **nucleus** of an atom. The nucleus is surrounded by even tinier particles called electrons. Electrons move around the nucleus in an area called the electron cloud.

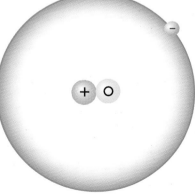

Protons have a positive electrical charge. Electrons have a negative electrical charge. Neutrons have no electrical charge. A whole atom has no electrical charge. Every atom contains an equal number of protons and electrons. The positive charge of each proton is balanced by the negative charge of each electron.

Elements

All matter is made of tiny particles called **atoms,** and there are many kinds of atoms. When a substance is made up of only one kind of atom, that substance is called an **element**. Elements are the simplest forms of matter. An element cannot be broken down into simpler substances. There are more

The Periodic Table

The **periodic table** is a chart that arranges all the known elements into groups. The groups have similar physical and

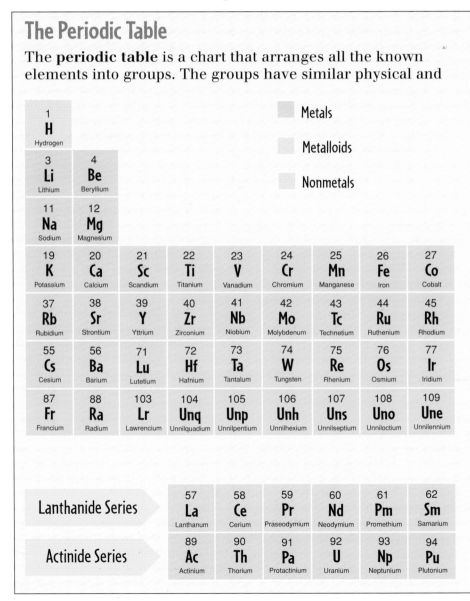

than 100 known elements. Oxygen, silver, lead, mercury, iron, and iodine are elements.

Properties of Elements

Each element has a characteristic number of protons, neutrons, and electrons in its atoms. The simplest of the atoms, the hydrogen atom, contains one proton in its nucleus. For

chemical properties. See how the nonmetals are grouped to the right of a zigzag line, metals are to the left of the line, and metalloids are along the line.

								2 **He** Helium
			5 **B** Boron	6 **C** Carbon	7 **N** Nitrogen	8 **O** Oxygen	9 **F** Fluorine	10 **Ne** Neon
			13 **Al** Aluminum	14 **Si** Silicon	15 **P** Phosphorus	16 **S** Sulfur	17 **Cl** Chlorine	18 **Ar** Argon
28 **Ni** Nickel	29 **Cu** Copper	30 **Zn** Zinc	31 **Ga** Gallium	32 **Ge** Germanium	33 **As** Arsenic	34 **Se** Selenium	35 **Br** Bromine	36 **Kr** Krypton
46 **Pd** Palladium	47 **Ag** Silver	48 **Cd** Cadmium	49 **In** Indium	50 **Sn** Tin	51 **Sb** Antimony	52 **Te** Tellurium	53 **I** Iodine	54 **Xe** Xenon
78 **Pt** Platinum	79 **Au** Gold	80 **Hg** Mercury	81 **Tl** Thallium	82 **Pb** Lead	83 **Bi** Bismuth	84 **Po** Polonium	85 **At** Astatine	86 **Rn** Radon

63 **Eu** Europium	64 **Gd** Gadolinium	65 **Tb** Terbium	66 **Dy** Dysprosium	67 **Ho** Holmium	68 **Er** Erbium	69 **Tm** Thulium	70 **Yb** Ytterbium
95 **Am** Americium	96 **Cm** Curium	97 **Bk** Berkelium	98 **Cf** Californium	99 **Es** Einsteinium	100 **Fm** Fermium	101 **Md** Mendelevium	102 **No** Nobelium

every proton in an atomic nucleus, there is one electron in the cloud surrounding the nucleus. So every hydrogen atom also contains a single electron.

Metals

Every element has its own physical and chemical properties. Most elements are **metals**. Metals are shiny solids that can be hammered into thin sheets or made into wires. Metals are good conductors of heat and electricity. They also tend to have a high density. Gold, silver, copper, aluminum, and iron are metals.

Iron is a metal.

Nonmetals

Another group of elements is the **nonmetals**. Nonmetals include gases, liquids, and solids. They are generally dull instead of shiny, and they do not conduct heat or electricity very well. They cannot be shaped into wires or thin sheets, and they tend to have a low density. The nonmetals include elements that are needed for life, such as carbon, oxygen, and nitrogen. Sulfur, neon gas, and iodine are also nonmetals.

Sulfur is a nonmetal.

Metalloids

Metalloids are solids that have properties of both metals and nonmetals. They conduct heat and electricity, but not as well as metals. Metalloids may be shiny or dull, and they can be shaped into sheets and wires. Metalloids include boron and arsenic.

Arsenic is a metalloid.

Molecules

A **molecule** is made up of two or more atoms. A molecule is the smallest particle of a substance that still has the properties of that substance. If the atoms of a molecule are separated, they no longer have the properties of the molecule. Instead, they will have the properties of the separate elements.

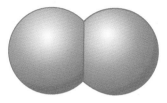

Sometimes all the atoms in a molecule are the same. For example, a molecule of hydrogen gas is made up of two hydrogen atoms.

Compounds

A **chemical compound** is a substance that contains only one type of molecule. A glass of pure water contains only water molecules. A box of pure cane sugar contains only sucrose molecules. Sucrose molecules are made up of carbon, hydrogen, and oxygen atoms.

It is impossible to separate the elements in a compound by physical changes. A compound has different properties from the elements that make it up.

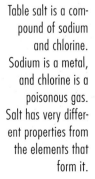

Table salt is a compound of sodium and chlorine. Sodium is a metal, and chlorine is a poisonous gas. Salt has very different properties from the elements that form it.

Some molecules include different kinds of atoms. When two hydrogen atoms and one oxygen atom are chemically combined, they form a molecule of water.

Combining Matter into Mixtures and Solutions

Mixtures

A **mixture** is a blend of two or more substances that have not been chemically combined. Each substance in a mixture keeps its own properties.

This shaker contains a mixture of water and glitter. When shaken, the two substances mix, but they do not combine. If you let it stand, the glitter will separate and settle to the bottom.

Both parts of this dessert are suspensions. Whipped cream is a mixture of gas particles (air) suspended in a liquid (cream). Pudding is a suspension of liquids in a solid.

Suspensions

A **suspension** is a mixture in which particles of one substance float, or are suspended, in another substance. Toothpaste contains tiny particles of chalk suspended in water and other liquids.

Solutions

A **solution** is a mixture that is formed when one substance dissolves in another. Ocean water is a solution containing many kinds of salts dissolved in water. Lemonade is a solution of lemon juice and sugar dissolved in water. In a solution, the molecules of each substance are evenly distributed.

The substance that is dissolved is called a **solute**. The solutes in a glass of lemonade are the lemon juice and the sugar. The substance that does the dissolving is called the **solvent.** Water is the solvent for most familiar solutions. That's why water is known as the "universal solvent."

Lemonade is a solution.

Force, Work, and Energy

Force

A **force** is a push or a pull that gives energy to an object. If the force is strong enough, it will make the object start moving, stop moving, or change direction while moving.

The force exerted by a softball pitcher's arm pushes the ball through the air toward the batter. The force of the batter's arm and bat changes the direction of the moving ball.

Gravity

Every object exerts a force on all the objects around it. This force is called **gravity**. The more mass an object has, the greater its gravitational force.

As a ball travels through the air, its mass pulls on the earth, and the earth's mass pulls on the ball. Since the earth's mass is larger than the ball's mass, the earth's gravitational force is larger. So the ball falls to the ground.

Inertia

Inertia is an object's resistance to changes in motion. The greater the mass of an object, the greater its inertia. The greater the inertia, the greater the force required to change the object's motion or position.

Imagine a box of bricks and an empty box the same size. It might take several strong people to lift the box of bricks. One person could lift the empty box. The box of bricks has more inertia, so it takes more force to move it.

Friction

Friction is a force that resists motion. Friction causes moving objects to slow down and stop. It exerts a force that is opposite to the direction of motion. The energy that is lost to friction often becomes heat. You can feel the heat of friction when you quickly rub your hands together.

Friction exists because objects are not perfectly smooth. The smoother an object, the less effect friction will have. Smooth ice does not have much friction. It does not slow down your forward motion much when you step on it, so you slip. A sidewalk has a rougher surface. Friction from the sidewalk resists your forward motion, and you're much less likely to slip.

Work

Work is done when a force moves an object over a distance. When you pick up a book, work is being done. You exert upward force on the book and move it to another place.

Work = force × distance

Work is the force applied to an object multiplied by the distance the object is moved. The applied force is equal to the mass of the object.

The farther you move an object, the more work is done. If you put a book on a high shelf, more work is done than if you put it on a desk. The more force you exert, the more work is done. If you pick up a stack of books instead of just one, you must exert more force to make the stack move. Again, more work is done.

Dylan is doing work by grasping a book (force) and lifting it up (distance). Erin has done more work than Dylan because she has picked up several books (more force). Tony has done more work than Dylan because he is lifting his book higher (more distance).

Machines and Work

If you wanted to dig a hole in the sand, would you use your fingers? Probably not. You would use a machine, such as a shovel. **Machines** make work easier to do. Simple machines are tools with only one or two parts. They can increase a force, change the direction of a force, or do both. Simple machines include the lever, the wheel and axle, and the inclined plane.

Lever

A **lever** is a rod or bar that turns or tilts around a fixed point. The fixed point is called the **fulcrum**. When a force is applied at one end of the lever, it moves a load at the other end.

FIRST-CLASS LEVER
In a **first-class lever**, the fulcrum is near the center. When work is done, both ends of the lever move equal distances. A first-class lever both increases force and changes the direction of force—a downward force moves the load upward.

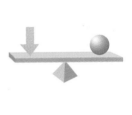

SECOND-CLASS LEVER
In a **second-class lever**, the fulcrum is at one end, and the force is applied at the opposite end. The load is near the center. Force is increased but the direction of the force is not changed—an upward force will move the load upward.

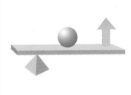

THIRD-CLASS LEVER
In a **third-class lever**, the fulcrum is at one end, and the load is at the opposite end. The force is applied somewhere in between. Force is increased, but the direction of force does not change.

Wheel and Axle

A **wheel** is a large circle that rotates around a smaller circle called an **axle**. Both wheel and axle rotate together. Doorknobs, steering wheels, and the wheels on automobiles are examples of wheels and axles. A wheel does not have to look like a car or a bicycle wheel. It just has to move in a circle. The handle of an old-fashioned well is a wheel.

A **pulley** is a wheel and axle with a rope passing over the wheel. A simple pulley does not increase force, but it does change the direction of force. A pulley makes it possible to raise a flag without climbing the flagpole. Two or more pulleys can be used together.

Gears are wheels and axles that work together to change the direction of force and increase the force. Gears have toothed edges that fit together. They are important parts of complex machines like automobiles, lawn mowers, and clocks.

The motion of the larger gear increases force by making the smaller gear move faster. The two gears move in opposite directions.

Inclined Plane

An **inclined plane** is a slanted surface that is used to raise or move objects. It increases the force but does not change the direction of the force.

Sliding a heavy weight up an inclined plane is easier than lifting it.

A **screw** is an inclined plane wound around a shaft. The screw both increases force and changes its direction. A turning motion pushes the screw down. Screws are used to open and close screw-cap jars and bottles. Nuts and bolts are another type of screw.

A **wedge** is made of two inclined planes. Where the planes meet, there is a sharp, narrow edge. The edge is used to cut or break. Wedges both increase force and change the direction of the force. Arrowheads and knives are wedges.

An ax head is a wedge. The downward force of the ax changes to an outward force that splits the log apart.

Complex Machines

A **complex machine** is made up of two or more simple machines. Scissors, can openers, and bicycles are complex machines. Cars and computers are also complex machines.

Mechanical Advantage

Machines make work easier by increasing force. **Mechanical advantage** is the amount by which a machine increases force. Friction decreases the mechanical advantage of a machine.

Mechanical Advantage = $\dfrac{\text{load}}{\text{effort force}}$

Mechanical advantage is calculated by dividing the amount of work done (the load) by the amount of effort put into the machine (the effort force).

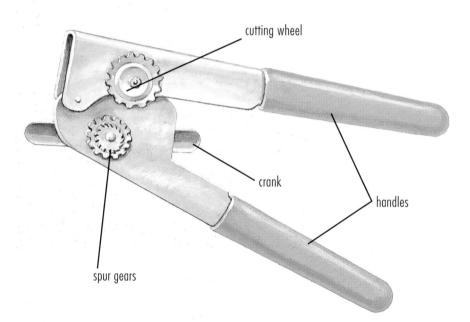

A can opener is a complex machine made up of two levers, several wheels and axles, and a wedge.

Efficiency

Efficiency is a comparison between the amount of work put into a machine and the amount of work the machine accomplishes. It describes how much energy a machine loses to friction. Efficiency is always expressed as a percentage.

Friction resists the motion of all moving objects. Machine parts moving against each other cause friction. Some of the effort force applied to any machine is lost to friction. It is never possible for a machine to be 100 percent efficient because some energy is always lost to friction. An efficient machine loses a small amount of energy to friction. An inefficient machine loses a lot of energy to friction.

Efficiency can be increased by adding a **lubricant**, such as grease or oil, to surfaces that rub together. Grease on a bicycle axle helps reduce the friction of the axle against the bicycle frame. Efficiency can also be increased by properly inflating tires. With properly inflated tires, a smaller part of the tire surface touches the road.

Work and Energy

Work cannot be done without energy. When work is done, energy moves from one object to another. For example, when a batter hits a baseball, the energy in the moving bat is transferred to the ball. When you move your arm up and down, energy from the food you eat is transferred to muscle cells.

Kinetic Energy

Kinetic energy is the energy of motion. When an object is in motion, it has kinetic energy. A ball rolling down a soccer field has kinetic energy. Water flowing from a faucet has kinetic energy. Even ketchup slowly oozing out of a bottle has kinetic energy.

The soccer ball moves when the player kicks it. The moving ball has kinetic energy.

Potential Energy

Potential energy is energy stored in objects that can be set into motion. It is energy that can be used to do work, but isn't being used yet. Potential energy changes into kinetic energy when motion begins. A ball held above the ground has potential energy. When the ball is dropped, the potential energy becomes kinetic energy.

The ball has potential energy. When the player drops it, the ball's potential energy will become kinetic energy. When the player kicks the ball, he will apply additional force to the ball and give it more kinetic energy.

Energy easily changes from kinetic to potential and back again. When a moving object stops its motion, its kinetic energy becomes potential energy. When the object begins moving again, its potential energy becomes kinetic energy.

Kinetic energy is changed into potential energy when a clown is pushed into a jack-in-the-box and the lid is closed to press down the spring. Potential energy is stored in the compressed spring. When the lid is released, the potential energy in the spring becomes kinetic energy again: The clown pops up.

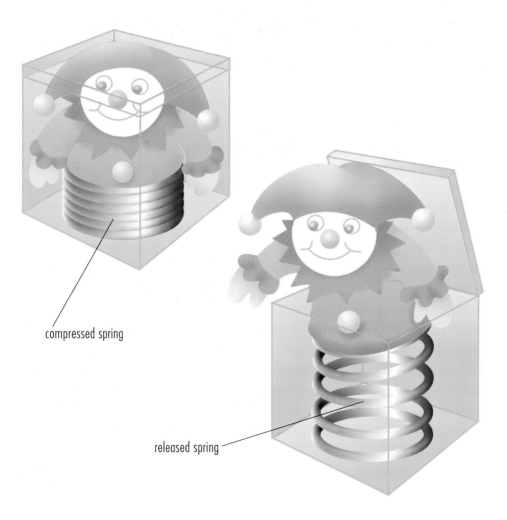

compressed spring

released spring

The Law of Conservation of Energy

Energy cannot be created or destroyed. Energy changes from kinetic to potential and back again, but it never disappears. Energy also has many forms, and it can change from one form to another.

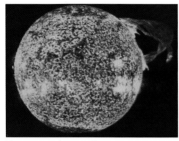

The sun produces radiant energy.

Radiant Energy

Radiant energy includes heat and light. Radiant energy can move through empty space. Sunshine and starlight are forms of radiant energy. So are the the heat and light given off by camp-fires and lightbulbs.

Chemical Energy

Chemical energy is energy that is released by a chemical reaction. The energy in food is released by the chemical reactions that take place during digestion. The fuel in a rocket engine contains chemical energy that is released when the fuel is burned.

Mechanical Energy

Mechanical energy is the energy that moves objects. Water flowing in a stream, runners in a race, and a spoon clattering to the floor are all examples of mechanical energy. So are chewing and the movement of muscles. In a car engine, the chemical energy released during the burning of gasoline changes into mechanical energy that moves the car. Mechanical energy lost to friction changes into heat energy.

The space shuttle uses chemical energy.

This runner uses mechanical energy to move.

Electrical Energy and Magnetism

Electricity

Electricity is caused by the motion of electrons. Electrons orbit around the nucleus of atoms. Sometimes they can move from one atom to another. Electricity is created when electrons move from atom to atom.

Electrical Charge

Electrical charge is a physical property of matter. The protons in the nucleus of an atom have a positive electrical charge (+). The neutrons in the nucleus of an atom have no electrical charge. The electrons that surround the atomic nucleus have a negative electrical charge (-).

Unlike charges attract—objects with different electrical charges move toward each other.

Atoms with more electrons than protons have a negative charge. Atoms with more protons than electrons have a positive charge. Atoms with an equal number of protons and electrons have no electrical charge.

Like charges repel—objects with the same electrical charge move away from each other.

An object containing electrically charged atoms is surrounded by an **electrical field**. This electrical field can exert a force on other objects.

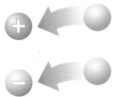

Charged objects attract uncharged objects—objects with no charge move toward charged objects.

Static Electricity

Static electricity is an electrical charge produced when an object gains or loses electrons. Most objects have no charge because their atoms have an equal number of protons and electrons. A static charge can be created by briskly rubbing two objects together. This causes electrons from one object to rub off onto the other.

Static electricity can jump from one object to another. When you walk across a wool rug on a cold, dry day, your body becomes negatively charged. When you touch a metal doorknob, the

If you rub a balloon against your hair, electrons will pass from your hair to the balloon. The balloon will have a negative charge, and your hair will have a positive charge. The opposite charges will make your hair and the balloon attract each other. They will also be attracted to objects with no charge, like your shirt.

extra electrons on your body jump to the metal. You feel an electric shock. You may even see a spark.

Lightning

Lightning is a form of static electricity. During a storm, electrical charges build up in clouds and on the ground. When these charges become large enough, they are released, or **discharged**. Electrons jump from negatively charged clouds to positively charged ground, creating a huge spark— a lightning bolt.

Electric Current

Electric current is the continuous flow of electrons through a conductor. (See page 70 for a definition of a conductor.) Electric current always flows in one direction.

Making Electricity

Electrons need a push to get moving. Devices that provide the energy for this push create electric current.

Battery

Batteries produce electric current by changing chemical energy to electrical energy. The device shown on the right is a dry-cell battery, the kind you might use in a flashlight. A dry-cell battery contains a metal rod surrounded by a special paste inside a zinc casing. The rod reacts chemically with the paste to release chemical energy. If you install the battery correctly, an electrical current will flow from the battery to the light and back again.

Generator

Generators produce electric current by changing mechanical energy to electrical energy. They use the power of moving water or steam to turn a wheel, called a turbine. The shaft, or axle, of the rotating turbine is attached to a coil of wire that spins around inside a magnetic field. The spinning creates a flow of electrons in the wire.

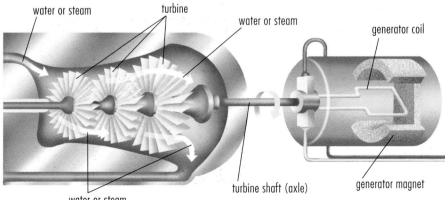

water or steam   turbine   water or steam   generator coil   turbine shaft (axle)   generator magnet   water or steam

Conductors

A **conductor** is any material through which an electric current can easily flow. Most metals are good conductors. Copper wire is the conductor most often used to carry electric current. Silver and aluminum are also good conductors.

Insulators

An **insulator** is a material that does not easily allow the flow of an electric current. Plastic, wood, and rubber are good insulators. The insulating material that covers an electric wire prevents the current from flowing out of the wire. It protects the user from being shocked.

The metal strands inside these wires are conductors that carry electric current. The plastic coating around the metal is an insulator that keeps electric current from passing through it.

Resistance

Anything that works against the free flow of electric current is **resistance**. A current flows more freely through a thick wire than a thin one, because the thicker wire has room for more electrons. Thin wire has a higher resistance than the thick wire. Copper is a better conductor than iron. Copper has a lower resistance. Resistance is measured in **ohms** (Ω).

Circuits

Current flows only when it can follow a closed path, called a **circuit**. A circuit needs an energy source, such as a battery, to start the electrical current. A wire connecting a light-bulb with the two terminals of a battery forms a complete circuit.

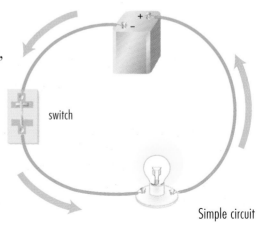

switch

Simple circuit

Series Circuits

A **series circuit** connects several objects, one after the other, in a single path. When the circuit is closed, current flows to all the objects along the path.

Series circuit

In a series circuit, if one of the lightbulbs burns out, the circuit will no longer be closed. The current will stop flowing, and all the bulbs will go out.

Parallel Circuits

A **parallel circuit** connects several objects in many paths. In a parallel circuit, each object is on its own path. If one of the lightbulbs burns out, the circuit is still closed, so the other bulbs will stay lit.

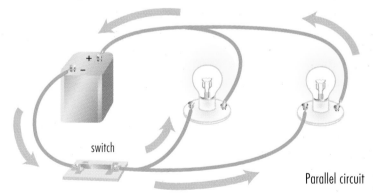

switch

Parallel circuit

Switches

Switches control the flow of electricity through a circuit. A switch is a conductor added to a circuit that can be connected or disconnected from the wire that carries the current. If the switch is closed, electricity can flow freely through the circuit. If the switch is open, the circuit is broken and electricity cannot flow through it.

Measuring Electricity

Voltage

Voltage is the amount of energy, or push, in the electrons flowing through a circuit. The **volt** (V) is the unit used to measure voltage.

Current

Current is the number of electrons flowing through a circuit. The **ampere** (amp) is the unit used to measure current.

Power

When an electric light is on, it uses **power.** Everything that uses electricity uses power. Power is a measure of the amount of work done in a set period of time. Electric power is measured in **watts** (W) or **kilowatts** (kW). A kilowatt is 1,000 watts. Power is calculated by multiplying volts times amperes.

Power = volts × amperes. The electric current used by small appliances in homes is about 120 volts. A lightbulb that uses ½ amp has a power of 60 watts.

This illustration represents voltage as electrons flow through a wire. Imagine that the large balls are electrons that carry a higher push, or voltage, and the small balls are electrons that carry a lower voltage.

This illustration represents current as electrons flow through a wire. The electrons carry the same voltage, but more of them flow through the top wire so it carries a greater current.

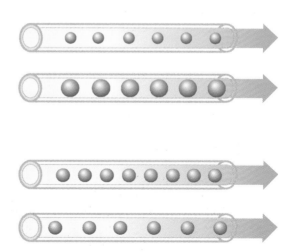

Magnetism

A **magnet** is a piece of metal that has a **magnetic field** around it. The magnetic field is invisible. Cobalt, nickel, and iron are metals that make good magnets. A lodestone is a natural magnet. Magnets attract some kinds of metals.

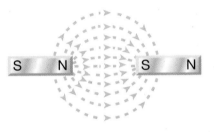

All magnets have two poles, a north pole and a south pole. The magnetic field is always strongest at the poles.

Earth is a huge magnet. Like all magnets, it has a north and south pole and is surrounded by a magnetic field. Earth's magnetic poles are not the same as its geographic poles. The geographic north and south pole are exactly at the top and bottom of earth's axis. The magnetic poles are near the geographic poles, but they are not at the same point.

Unlike magnetic poles attract one another.

A compass is a needle-shaped magnet used to locate the nearest magnetic pole. The north pole of the earth attracts the south pole of the compass needle, and the south pole of the earth attracts the north pole of the compass needle.

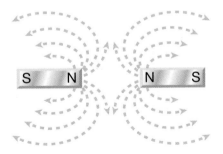

Like magnetic poles repel one another.

It is possible to go farther north than the magnetic north pole or farther south than the magnetic south pole. If you stand at the geographic north pole, your compass needle will point south instead of north.

Electricity and Magnetism

Electricity and magnetism are related. An electric current flowing through a wire creates a magnetic field around the wire. When the current stops, the magnetic field disappears.

Magnets in a TV focus electrons at the screen to produce the picture.

Electromagnets

An **electromagnet** is made by coiling a wire around a piece of iron. When current flows through the wire, the iron becomes a magnet. When the current stops, the iron is no longer magnetized.

VCRs use magnetism to store images on tape and convert them to pictures.

Electromagnets are used in electric motors to change electric energy into mechanical energy. Giant electromagnets are used to separate metals at recycling centers. Electromagnets are also used in many everyday devices, including doorbells, telephones, and tape recorders.

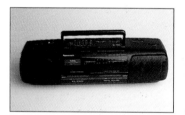

Speakers use magnets to convert electrical impulses to sound.

When electrons flow through a wire, their movement creates a magnetic field around the wire.

Light Energy

Light in Motion

Light is a form of radiant energy. Light travels through air and through empty space. It can even travel through some solid objects.

Sources of Light

The shining full moon is not a source of light. The moon is bright because it reflects the sun's rays.

A light source is any object that gives off its own light. The sun and stars, burning candles, and electric lamps are sources of light. Lightbulbs and campfires produce light as a result of being heated. The thin filament in a lightbulb heats up when electricity flows through it. The fuel in a fire releases light when it burns. A firefly lights up as a result of chemical reactions taking place inside its body.

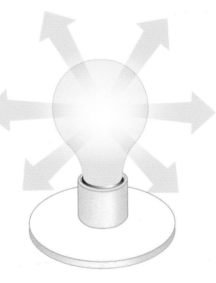

Rays of light travel out from their source in a straight line. As rays of light move away from their source, they spread out and become weaker.

Light and Objects

When light hits matter, it can be transmitted, reflected, or absorbed. See page 81 to find out about objects that absorb light.

Transmitted Light

Some objects allow light to pass through them. These objects transmit light.

Transparent objects include clear glass, plastic, and water. A transparent object allows almost all the

Clear glass is transparent.

light that strikes it to pass through. **Translucent** objects include colored glass, frosted glass, waxed paper, and thin, light-colored cloth. A translucent object allows some of the light that strikes it to pass through.

An **opaque** object does not transmit light at all. None of the light that strikes it is allowed to pass through.

Frosted glass is translucent.

When an opaque object gets in the way of light rays, it casts a shadow. A shadow is the absence of light.

Wood is opaque.

This fence casts a shadow because it blocks the path of the sunlight.

Reflected Light

Some of the light that strikes an object bounces off the object and travels back the way it came. Light that bounces back is **reflected** light. Opaque objects reflect most of the light that strikes them. You can see the moon in the sky because it reflects the sun's light. Transparent objects reflect very little of the light that strikes them.

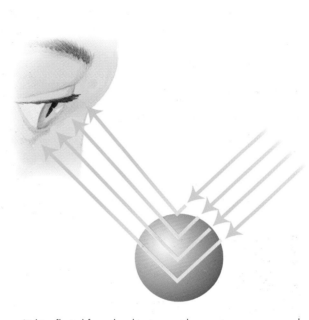

Light reflected from the objects around you enters your eyes and forms the images you see.

Mirrors Are Reflectors

The surface of a mirror is so shiny that it reflects almost all the light that strikes it. Because the mirror is smooth and flat, light rays bounce off the glass at the same angle they strike it. The result is a clear reflected image. The surface of a clear, still pool can also produce a clear reflected image.

When you look into a mirror, the light reflected from it enters your eyes. The reflected light rays seem to come from behind the mirror.

Curved Reflectors

Not all mirrors are flat. Curved mirrors have special purposes.

Concave Mirrors

A curved mirror with a surface that bends inward—"caves in"—is a **concave** mirror. The shiny reflector that surrounds the bulb of a flashlight or the headlight of a car is a concave mirror. The inside of a shiny metal bowl or spoon can serve as a concave mirror.

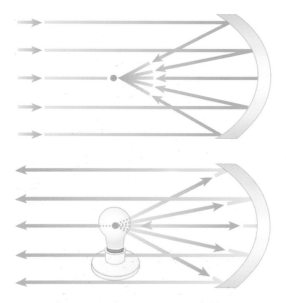

Light rays that strike the surface of a concave mirror are reflected back to a single point. This point is called the **focal point**.

If a light is placed at the focal point of a concave mirror, the rays will be reflected straight out. Lightbulbs in spotlights and flashlights are placed at the focal point of a concave mirror. The reflected rays add to the brightness of the light.

Convex Mirrors

A curved mirror with a surface that bends outward is a **convex** mirror. The rounded portion of the side view mirror on a car or truck is a convex mirror. A shiny metal ball or the outside of a metal spoon or bowl can be used as a convex mirror.

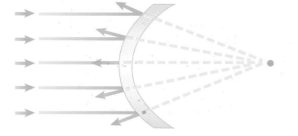

Light rays striking a convex mirror spread out when they are reflected back. A convex mirror will reflect light rays from a larger area than a flat mirror will.

Bending Light–Refraction

Light rays travel straight out from their source through air or empty space. But light rays bend if they pass through glass, water, or other transparent objects. The bending of light is called **refraction**.

When light is bent, it changes speed. Light travels through empty space at 300,000 kilometers (186,000 miles) per second. When light travels through matter—such as air or water or glass—it slows down. The speed of light depends on the density of the matter the light is traveling through. Light slows down when it passes from a less dense medium into a more dense medium. It speeds up when it passes from a more dense medium into a less dense medium.

When light rays bend, it can make objects look funny. Think of what happens when you look at an object—like a pencil or your fingers— through a glass of water. The objects might look as if they are wavy or as if they are broken into two pieces. That's because light moves more slowly through water than it does through air. This change in speed causes the light to bend, and the bending makes the objects appear distorted.

Lenses Bend Light

Lenses are pieces of glass specially shaped to bend light in certain ways. Magnifying glasses, microscopes, and telescopes use lenses to make objects appear larger. Slide projectors and movie projectors use lenses to display enlarged images on a surface.

Convex Lens

A **convex lens** is shaped so that the glass is thicker in the center and thinner at the edges. Light rays that enter a convex lens bend in toward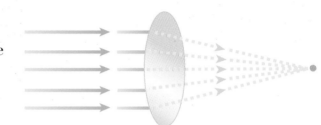

A convex lens focuses light toward a single point.

the center of the lens. The rays come together on the other side of the lens at a point called the **focal point.**

Glasses for farsighted people have convex lenses. Farsighted people have a hard time seeing objects that are close. The lenses make a close-up image seem to come from farther away.

Concave Lens

A **concave lens** is shaped so that the glass is thinner in the center and thicker at the edges. Light rays that pass through a concave lens bend out away from the center of the lens.

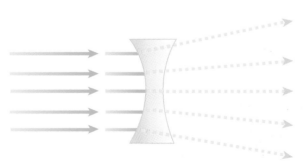

Glasses for nearsighted people have concave lenses. Nearsighted people have a hard time seeing objects that are far away. The lenses make distant objects look closer.

A concave lens bends light outward.

Light and Color

Rainbow

The light cast by the sun appears to be white, or colorless. But sunshine actually contains all the colors of the rainbow.

A **prism** is a type of lens. A prism bends light so that the rays of each color are separated from one another. A rainbow appears when water droplets in the sky act as prisms.

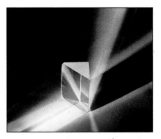

Glass prism

Seeing Colors

Objects absorb some colors of light and reflect others. The color you see is the color that is reflected from the object. You don't see the colors that are absorbed by the object. Grass looks green because it absorbs the other colors of light and reflects the green light back to your eyes.

Red objects reflect red light rays and absorb all others.

Sound Energy

Sound Is Motion

Sound is produced when energy causes objects to vibrate. Vibrating objects move back and forth very rapidly. Each back-and-forth motion forms a sound wave. Sound waves move out from their source like ripples spreading out from a stone thrown into a pond.

compression

rarefication

sound wave

How You Hear Sound

Sound waves move through the air. When sound waves from a ringing bell reach your ear, they make your eardrum vibrate the same way the bell is vibrating. The vibrating eardrum sends messages to your brain, and you hear the bell.

A ringing bell creates sound waves. Each back-and-forth vibration of the bell alternately squeezes together and stretches apart the air molecules around the bell. The squeezed-together molecules are **compressed**. The stretched-apart molecules are **rarefied.** Each set of compressed and rarefied air molecules represents a **sound wave**. A ringing bell sets off hundreds of sound waves each second.

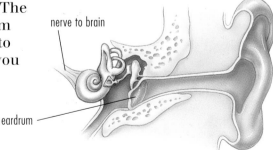

nerve to brain

eardrum

Making Sound

The strings of a violin vibrate when a bow is drawn across them.

The energy of any kind of vibrating matter makes sound. For example, your voice is made up of sound waves created by the vibrations of the vocal cords in your throat. You can feel the vibrations of your voice by putting your hand on your throat while speaking or singing.

Musical instruments create sound in a variety of ways. For instance, pressing the key of a piano causes a hammer to strike a string inside the piano. The vibrations of the string make the sound we hear.

Blowing into an opening at one end of a saxophone or other wind instrument sets up vibrations in the column of air inside the instrument.

Striking the metal bar of a xylophone causes the bar to vibrate. The vibrating bar creates vibrations in the air inside the tube below. The vibrations in the tube make the sound louder.

Sound and Matter

Without matter, there can be no sound. Sound cannot move through empty space, because there are no particles to conduct the sound from its source to the ear. Sound waves can move through air, water, wood, metal, and many other kinds of matter. The matter that a sound wave travels through is called the **medium**. The greater the density of the medium, the better the sound travels. Sound travels more easily through liquids and solids than it does through air and other gases. The songs of whales carry for miles through the ocean but can be heard for only a short distance through the air.

(A) Tie one end of a two-foot string to the hook of a metal coat hanger and wrap the other end of the string around one finger. Hold the hanger away from you and tap it with a pencil. The sound of the vibrating metal is carried through the air to your ears.

Measuring Sound

Intensity is the loudness or soft-ness of a sound. The intensity of a sound is measured in **decibels**. A whisper is about 15 decibels. A vacuum cleaner is about 80 decibels.

The **pitch** of a sound is its high-ness or lowness. Pitch depends on **frequency**. Frequency is the number of times the sound source vibrates in one second. Each vibration is one back-and-forth motion, or one **cycle**. Frequency is measured in cycles per second. The lowest note on a piano vibrates about 28 times— or 28 cycles—per second. The highest note vibrates at more than 4,200 cycles per second.

(B) Press the finger with the string against the opening of one ear. Do not put your finger or the string in your ear. Now tap the hanger again. The sound is even stronger, because sound travels more easily through the solid string than through the air.

Echoes

An **echo** is a sound reflected off an object. Hard surfaces make better echoes than soft surfaces.

Bats, dolphins, and some other animals use a kind of echo called **sonar** to find their way and locate prey in the dark. Bats have very high-pitched voices that humans cannot hear. The bat sends out bursts of sound and listens for echoes. With its keen sense of hearing, the bat hears the echoes of its voice reflecting off walls, trees, insects, or other bats.

Sound and Light

Sound and light energy have important differences. Sound is a form of mechanical energy. Light is a form of radiant energy. Sound travels about 330 meters per second. Light travels much faster, at about 300,000,000 meters per second. Sound waves can bend around solid objects. Light waves bend only when they pass through certain substances. That's why you can hear around the corner, but you can't see around the corner.

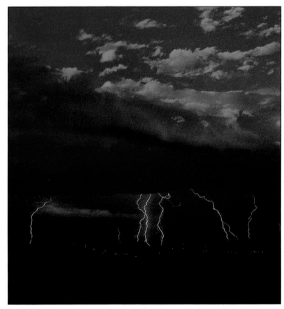

You often see a bolt of lightning before you hear the thunderclap. Because light travels faster than sound, the light from the lightning reaches you before the sound does.

Sound and light are also similar in many ways. Both spread out in all directions from their source. Both decrease in intensity as they get farther from their source. And sound and light can both be reflected.

Heat Energy

Heat Is Motion

Like light, **heat** is a form of energy. It is the kinetic energy of atoms and molecules in constant motion. Radiation from the sun includes heat as well as light. Heat is produced when fuel is burned. Even friction produces heat. Heat is also produced by the friction of an electric current passing through a wire. A lightbulb produces both light and heat.

The more energy is present, the faster atoms and molecules move. An object warms up as its atoms and molecules move faster. The energy can come from a chemical reaction, friction, or even heat from another object. Heat energy moves from something that is hot to something that is less hot.

When wood fuel burns, both light and heat energy are produced.

When heat is added to an object, it warms up. The motion of its atoms and molecules speeds up.

When heat is taken from an object, it cools down. The motion of its atoms and molecules slows down.

Expansion

Heat energy makes molecules move faster. Faster molecules bump together more often and with more energy, so they push away from each other. When an object gets hotter, its molecules move away from each other. Hot objects **expand**, or take up more space.

Contraction

Colder molecules move slower. Slower molecules bump into each other less often, so they don't push away from each other as much. When an object gets colder, its molecules get closer together. Cold objects **contract**, or take up less space.

If you live in a climate with hot summers and cold winters, you may have seen one effect of expansion and contraction. Perhaps there is a door in your house that opens and closes easily in winter but sticks in its frame in the summer. Summer's heat makes the door expand. When it is a little larger, it does not fit well in its frame.

Heat and Temperature

Temperature is a measure of how fast an object's molecules are moving. Thermometers are devices used to measure temperature. The unit used to measure temperature is the **degree**.

Temperature is used to measure heat. The temperature tells you how hot or cold it is outdoors. A doctor finds out if a patient has a fever by taking his or her temperature. A cook sets the temperature of the oven so food will bake properly.

Temperature Scales

The degrees on a thermometer are marked with a series of numbers, called a **scale**. There are three different temperature scales that use different numbers to measure temperature.

The **Fahrenheit** scale is the temperature scale most widely used in the United States. The **Celsius** scale is an international scale used by people in many countries of the world, and by most scientists. The **Kelvin** scale is used by scientists who work with very low temperatures.

Fahrenheit	Celsius	Kelvin	
212°	100°	373°	boiling point of water
32°	0°	273°	freezing point of water
–460°	–273°	0°	absolute zero

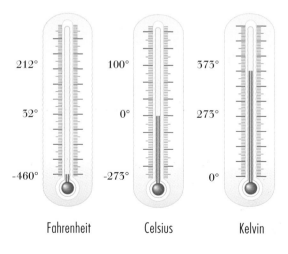

Fahrenheit   Celsius   Kelvin

The boiling point of water is the temperature at which liquid water turns to steam. The freezing point of water is the temperature at which liquid water turns to ice. Absolute zero is the temperature at which atoms do not move at all—they have no kinetic energy.

How Heat Moves

Heat flows from one object to another. The flow of heat is sometimes called **heat transfer**. Heat can move in three different ways.

Radiation is heat energy that flows through space. Heat can radiate through empty space that contains no matter at all. Heat from the sun radiates through empty space to reach earth. Heat from a fireplace or a candle radiates outward.

Conduction is heat energy that flows from the molecules of a warmer object to the molecules of a cooler object. Heat is conducted between objects that touch.

Convection is the circular movement of heat. It takes place only in liquids and gases. Heat causes molecules in liquids or gases to move upward. As molecules are heated, they move faster and push away from each other, the liquid or gas expands and becomes less dense. As the matter becomes less dense, the molecules rise. When the liquid or gas loses heat, it becomes more dense again and sinks down.

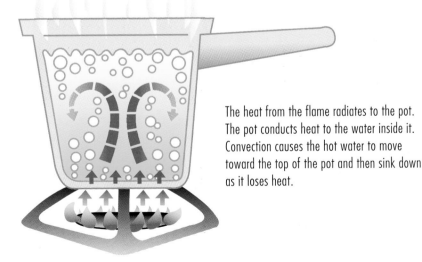

The heat from the flame radiates to the pot. The pot conducts heat to the water inside it. Convection causes the hot water to move toward the top of the pot and then sink down as it loses heat.

Heat and Electricity

Heat and electricity have important similarities. Both can be conducted by some materials. Metals are good conductors of both heat and electricity. Paper, rubber, and plastics are insulators that do not conduct heat or electricity very well.

Electricity produces heat. When electric current passes through a wire, the resistance of the wire creates friction. (See page 70 for a definition of resistance.) The friction creates heat. The coils of a toaster glow with heat produced by electrical resistance.

Nuclear Energy

Heat, light, and other forms of radiant energy are released when atomic nuclei are split apart or fused together.

Nuclear fission is the splitting apart of atomic nuclei. The forces that hold the nucleus of an atom together are extremely strong. When an atom is split, a huge amount of energy is released. Nuclear power plants use the heat produced by nuclear fission to turn turbines and produce electricity.

Nuclear fusion forces protons and neutrons together to create new atomic nuclei. This process can produce enormous amounts of energy. Nuclear fusion takes place in the sun and other stars. We have not yet found a way to produce power we can use through nuclear fusion.

Stars are giant nuclear furnaces that produce light, heat, X rays, radio waves, and other forms of radiant energy.

The Earth Below

Earth's Composition

Earth is made up of land, water, and air. The water is called the **hydrosphere**. The air that surrounds the earth is the **atmosphere**. The land is called the **lithosphere**. The lithosphere is made up of several layers.

At the center of the earth is a very hot core. The **inner core** is solid nickel and iron. Temperatures here reach 5,000° Celsius (9,000° Fahrenheit). Nickel and iron are usually molten, or liquid, at these temperatures. But the inner core is under tremendous pressure from the weight of the rock above it. This weight presses the molten nickel and iron into a dense, solid mass. The **outer core** is liquid nickel and iron. Temperatures in the outer core range from 2,200° to 5,000° Celsius (4,000° to 9,000° Fahrenheit).

The **mantle,** which surrounds the core, is the lithosphere's thickest layer. It is made of silicon, magnesium, iron, oxygen, and a few other elements. The temperature of the mantle ranges from about 870° to about 2,200° Celsius (1,600° to 4,000° Fahrenheit). The temperature is highest in the lower mantle near the core. High temperatures and pressures in the mantle make it possible for molten rock to flow very slowly— like thick, moist clay. The moving rock flows in **convection currents** that affect the earth's crust.

The **crust** is the thinnest, outermost layer of the lithosphere. If the earth were compared to an apple or a peach, the crust would be as thin as the skin of the fruit. The crust that lies below land masses is about 32 kilometers (20 miles) thick. It can be much thicker in regions covered by high mountains. Under the oceans, the crust may be only about eight to ten kilometers (five to six miles) thick. All life on earth is limited to the crust and the water or air that lies just above the crust.

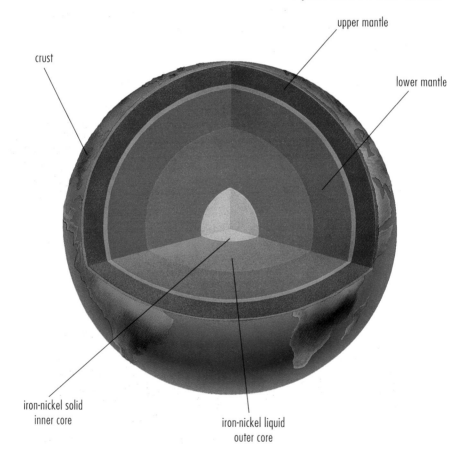

upper mantle

crust

lower mantle

iron-nickel solid
inner core

iron-nickel liquid
outer core

Plate Tectonics

Continents are the portions of earth's crust that rise above the ocean's surface. It's hard to imagine the size, shape, and location of the continents changing. But they have actually been drifting over earth's surface for about 300 million years. This movement is called **continental drift**.

Plate tectonics is the theory scientists use to explain continental drift. According to the theory, earth's crust is made up of several pieces, called **plates**. These plates float on top of the molten mantle. The edges of the plates are constantly being pushed together and pulled apart.

Millions of years ago, all the continents were grouped together in one huge landmass. This ancient continent is known as **Pangaea.** Over time, parts of Pangaea broke off and drifted away from each other. They now form today's continents, and the continents are still slowly moving over earth's surface.

Pangaea

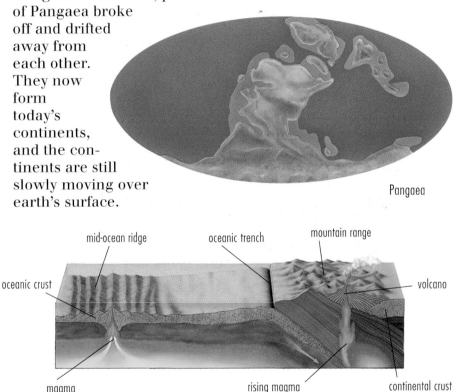

In some areas, plates are spreading apart. There, molten rock, or **magma**, from the mantle is forced up through the cracks between the plates. The magma slowly cools and attaches itself to the crust. **Ridges** form on the ocean floor between spreading plates. In some areas, plates crash into each other. There, the edge of one plate is pushed under the edge of the other. The part of the crust that is pushed down heats up and melts. It becomes part of the mantle. **Trenches** and **mountain ranges** are formed where plates crash into each other.

Earthquakes

Earthquakes take place at breaks in earth's crust. These breaks are called **faults**. Faults are caused by the pushing and pulling forces of plate movement. An earthquake occurs when the rocks on the two sides of an earthquake fault move against each other. The energy released by this motion shakes the ground.

Earthquake Faults

Normal Fault

The two sides of the fault are pulled apart. One side moves down. The other side may form a mountain range.

Reverse Fault

The two sides of the fault are pushed together. One side moves up. The highest mountains on earth, the Himalayas, were formed in part by reverse faults.

Strike-Slip Fault

The two sides of the fault slide past each other. California's famous San Andreas fault is a strike-slip fault.

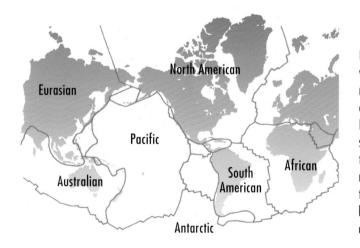

Earthquakes and volcanoes happen most often near the edges of the plates. Plate boundaries shown in red on this map are the regions that have the highest numbers of earthquakes and volcanoes.

Volcanoes

Volcanoes form where molten rock from the mantle makes its way up through earth's crust. Volcanoes most often form at the edges of tectonic plates. They are also found in areas where the crust is especially thin.

Sudden, violent volcanic eruptions happen when gases and magma explode into the air. The molten rock is thrown high into the sky. It comes back down as ash, cinders, and rock. Explosive eruptions form steep-sided mountains called **cinder cones**.

Slow, quiet eruptions happen when molten lava slowly oozes from openings in earth's crust. These lava flows cover large areas and create gently sloped mountains called **shield volcanoes**.

Some volcanoes are formed by alternating explosive and quiet eruptions. Explosive eruptions form cinder cones. The cinder cones are then covered up by lava flows. These alternating layers create some of the tallest volcanoes in the world.

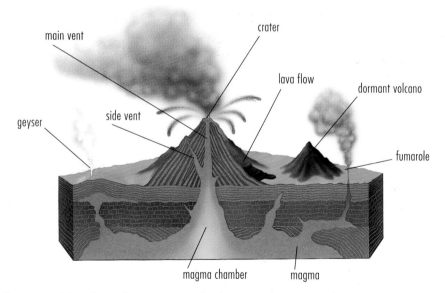

Magma is molten rock. It collects in **magma chambers** in earth's crust. A **volcanic eruption** takes place when the magma from the magma chamber works its way to the surface. Once magma flows out onto the earth's surface, it is called **lava**.

Formation of Rocks

All rocks in earth's crust can be separated into three types, depending on how the rock was formed.

Igneous Rocks

Granite

Igneous rocks are formed when magma or lava cools and becomes solid.

Intrusive igneous rocks are formed by magma that cools below earth's surface. Granite is a hard, light-colored rock that contains several different kinds of crystals. Granite is often used as a building material. Large crystals of amethysts, quartz, and other minerals form when underground magma cools very slowly. These crystals are often used in making jewelry.

Extrusive igneous rocks are formed by lava that cools on the surface. Pumice is a soft, porous rock riddled with tiny holes. These holes were formed by bubbles of gas that were trapped

Pumice

in quickly cooling lava. Some pumice is light enough to float. Because of its rough texture, pumice is used for grinding, polishing, and smoothing surfaces. Obsidian is hard, shiny, and usually black. It has a texture like glass. Obsidian forms when very thick lava cools very quickly. Because it has very sharp edges when broken, prehistoric people used obsidian for cutting.

Obsidian

cooling lava

trapped magma

Sedimentary Rocks

Sedimentary rocks are made of layers of materials that have been squeezed or cemented together. These materials include clay, sand, mud, small rocks, fossils, and minerals. Sedimentary rocks are grouped by how they are formed.

Some sedimentary rocks are made of bits and pieces that have been broken off other rocks. Sandstone is formed from layer after layer of sand grains that are deposited on the ground by wind or water. As one layer is deposited on top of another, the weight of the upper layers presses down on the layers below. Over time, the lowest layers are squeezed together until they become rock. Shale is formed much like sandstone, but it is made of layers of mud or dust. Small rocks and fossils are often part of sedimentary rocks.

Sandstone

Shale

Other sedimentary rocks are formed from minerals that were once dissolved in water. When water is heated, it turns into vapor, or **evaporates**. When the water evaporates, mineral deposits are left behind. Rock salt is made of minerals left behind by evaporating salt water. Rock formations in caves are formed by water that drips down from the cave ceiling. As the water evaporates, limestone deposits are left behind.

Salt

Limestone

Metamorphic Rocks

Metamorphic rocks are formed far below the surface. Sometimes a rock is buried deep in the earth. High temperatures make the rock softer. The weight of tons of material above it squeezes and folds the rock. When the rock cools and hardens once again, it has been changed from one type of rock to another.

Limestone is a sedimentary rock. It can turn into marble, a metamorphic rock. To make marble, limestone must be exposed to the heat of magma pushing up from below and the pressure of rock pushing down from above. The heat and pressure cause both physical and chemical changes in the limestone to make marble.

limestone

marble

magma

Speckled granite turns into a metamorphic rock called gneiss. Granite is an igneous

Granite

Gneiss

rock containing several different minerals. High pressure and heat squeeze these minerals tightly together to make the bands of color in the gneiss.

The Rock Cycle

Earth's crust is always changing. The tectonic plates are constantly moving. They can bump, slide, or spread apart. They pull rocks down toward the mantle. They push other rocks up toward the surface. Lava flowing from volcanoes forms new rock as it cools. Wind and rain break up rocks as soon as they form on the surface. Because of these movements, the rock that makes up the crust is constantly changing from one form to another. These changes are known as the **rock cycle**.

sedimentary rock

break up of rocks

metamorphic rock

igneous rock

volcanic activity

Rocks are broken into smaller and smaller pieces by many forces. Wind, rain, and freezing and thawing are some of these forces. The pieces are washed downhill by flowing water and deposited into layers that may become sedimentary rock. Layers of sedimentary rock may also bury other rocks.

Buried rock moves downward into the crust. It is heated from below and pressed down from above. The changes caused by heat and pressure form metamorphic rocks.

If the rock becomes hot enough, it melts into magma. The melted rock moves up toward the surface. It cools and hardens into igneous rock.

Breaking Down Rocks

Rocks are broken apart by a process called **weathering**. There are two types of weathering.

Plants can cause physical weathering.

Physical weathering breaks down rock without changing its chemical properties. The slow growth of tree roots can gradually split rocks apart. Flowing water often carries with it tiny particles of sand that can gradually wear away the rock as they flow against it. Waves crashing against a beach grind rocks and shells into smaller and smaller particles. Wind can cause physical weathering by gradually wearing away the surface of rocks.

Chemical weathering breaks down rock by changing the rock's chemical properties. Many of the minerals that make up rock will dissolve in water. When the water flows away, it leaves behind rocks that contain fewer minerals. The oxygen and carbon dioxide in air can also react with rock to cause chemical changes. Carbon dioxide dissolves in rain to form a weak acid. The acid reacts with rock. Oxygen combines with iron in some types of rock. This chemical reaction changes the iron to iron oxide, or rust.

Particles in water can cause physical weathering.

Erosion

Once rocks have been broken down, the smaller pieces are moved from place to place in a process called **erosion**. When the movement stops, the particles are left in a new location.

Dust, sand, and small pieces of rock can be picked up by strong winds. When the wind slows or stops, the particles drop to the ground. Flowing water also picks up bits of rock and carries them along. These rocks are dropped wherever the water stops or slows.

A glacier can travel about three feet per day, scraping the rock beneath it and changing the landscape. Sometimes, a glacier melts after thousands of years and leaves behind new valleys, lakes, rivers, or waterfalls.

Glaciers are frozen, slow-moving rivers of ice. As glacier ice scrapes against rock and soil, it picks up pieces. These pieces can range in size from dust grains to boulders. A glacier can carry its load of rock for hundreds of miles.

Sediments are the particles left behind by wind, flowing water, or glacial ice. Sedimentary rock forms when layer after layer of sediment is deposited in an area.

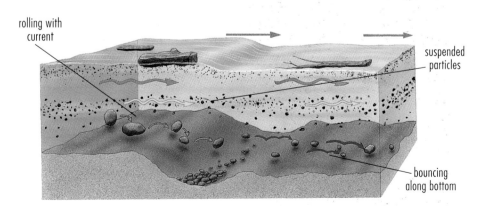

Rocks become rounded as they tumble along in a river or stream. Even as erosion moves them along, weathering wears off their sharp edges.

Fossils

Sediments may be left on top of the bodies of dead organisms. Under certain conditions, hard parts such as shell, bone, or wood may become **fossils**. Fossils can form when body parts are replaced by minerals. They also form when the body leaves its shape in sediments as they harden into rock.

Trilobites like these became extinct 225 million years ago.

By studying fossil remains, scientists are able to learn a great deal about organisms that lived many years ago. They can also learn about the climate, geology, and other conditions in the environment at the time the organisms were alive.

Fossil wood is sometimes called petrified wood.

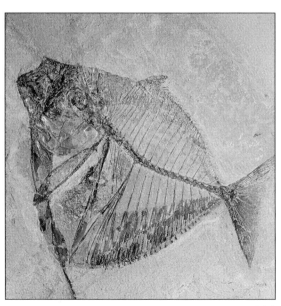

Fossil fish

Formation of Soil

Soil is formed from weathered rock that has been broken down into very tiny particles. Soil also contains **humus**. Humus is made of the partially decayed bodies of dead organisms. Soils are classified by their particle size and the amount of humus they contain.

Sandy soils have fairly large particles. Water and nutrients drain quickly through the large spaces between the particles. Sandy soils are found in deserts and near bodies of water.

Silty soils have medium-sized particles. Silty soil particles are smaller than sand grains and larger than clay particles.

Clay soils have small, tightly packed particles. Water does not easily drain through the tiny spaces between clay particles. Plants do not grow easily in clay soil.

Loamy soils contain large amounts of humus. Humus adds valuable nutrients to sandy, silty, or clay soils. Humus also improves soil texture and helps plants grow. Loamy soils absorb water well but allow excess water to drain away. Most plants grow easily in loamy soil.

Soil formation begins with the weathering of rock. Larger pieces are broken down into smaller and smaller fragments, until soil particles are formed. Plants that take root in the soil help form more soil. Their roots cause physical weathering. Some plants, including lichens and moss, give off acids that cause chemical weathering. The decaying bodies of dead plants add humus to the soil. Over time, a thick layer of soil develops.

The Earth Above

The Ocean Floor

Mountains and valleys, hills and plains are familiar features of the landscape above water. Similar features are also found on the ocean floor.

Rift valleys and mid-ocean ridges occur where two tectonic plates are spreading apart. They are formed by magma that seeps up into the cracks between spreading plates.

At the edge of the shore, the **continental shelf** slants gently down toward the ocean center.

At the edge of the continental shelf is a steeply sloped region called the **continental slope.**

Flat regions of the ocean floor are called **abyssal plains.**

Ocean **trenches** are long, deep, narrow canyons that occur where one tectonic plate slides beneath another.

At the bottom of the continental slope lies the **ocean floor.**

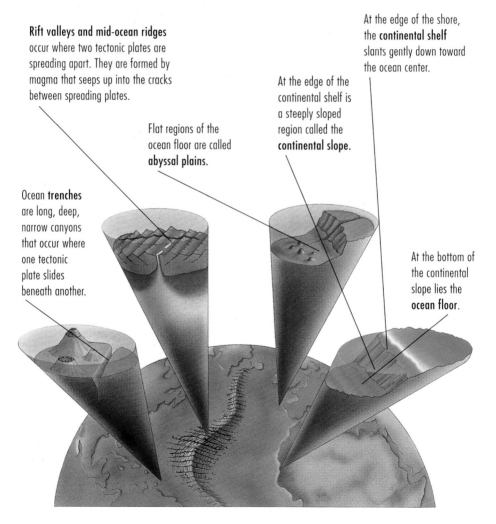

Ocean Movements

Most **waves** are caused by wind blowing across the surface of the water. The stronger the wind, the higher the waves.

Wind also causes ocean **currents**. The water in an ocean current flows in a particular direction. Warm currents travel away from the equator, and cold currents travel back toward it. Ocean currents travel great distances and can have a strong effect on the weather.

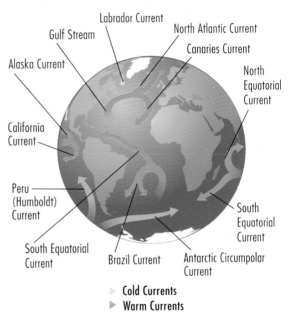

Labrador Current

Gulf Stream

North Atlantic Current

Canaries Current

Alaska Current

North Equatorial Current

California Current

Peru (Humboldt) Current

South Equatorial Current

Brazil Current

Antarctic Circumpolar Current

South Equatorial Current

▷ Cold Currents
▶ Warm Currents

Tides

If you have spent time by the seashore, you may have noticed that at certain times of day, the water is higher on the beach than at other times. These regular changes in the ocean's water level are called **tides.**

The gravitational pull of the moon causes the water in the ocean to rise and fall. Along most shorelines, there are two low tides and two high tides every day. At high tide, ocean water moves higher up onto shore. At low tide, the water stays farther back.

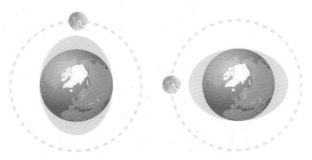

The moon's gravity pulls on both the earth and the ocean. The ocean under the moon bulges toward it. The ocean on the opposite side of earth also bulges out because of earth's spin. The bulges are areas of high tide. As the moon orbits the earth, the tidal bulges move along with it.

The Atmosphere

Air is a mixture of gases that includes nitrogen, oxygen, carbon dioxide, and water vapor. The atmosphere can be divided into five major layers. Each layer has a characteristic temperature range and altitude. As you move up from earth's surface, the density of the atmosphere decreases.

The **troposphere** is closest to earth's surface. It contains 75 percent of the gases in the atmosphere. All weather takes place in the troposphere.

The **stratosphere** contains the **ozone layer**. Ozone is a gas that filters harmful rays from the sun. The stratosphere also contains a strong wind current, called the **jet stream**. The jet stream helps form weather patterns.

The **mesosphere** is the coldest part of the atmosphere. Most meteors that enter the atmosphere from space burn up in the mesosphere. Radio waves travel through the mesosphere.

Temperatures in the **thermosphere** are very high. The air is thin, and air molecules are few and far apart.

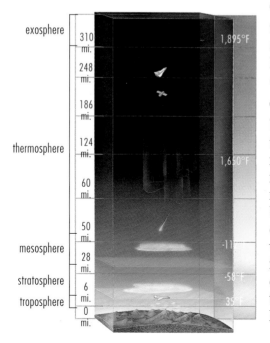

The **exosphere** extends for thousands of kilometers above earth's surface. Beyond the exosphere lies outer space.

The **ionosphere** is the boundary between the thermosphere and the mesosphere. Air molecules in the ionosphere absorb radiation from the sun and become charged particles called **ions**. AM radio waves bounce off the ionosphere and back to earth, making it possible to transmit radio signals over long distances.

Air Pressure

The weight of the atmosphere presses down on everything on earth's surface, including land, water, and living things. The force of the air's weight is called **air pressure**. Air pressure depends on density—the denser the air, the greater the air pressure. (See page 47 for information about density.) Air pressure in the thin air at the tops of mountains is lower than air pressure at sea level.

Heating the Earth–The Greenhouse Effect

Earth's air, water, and land absorb radiant energy from the sun. (To find out more about radiant energy, see page 66.) Some of the energy from the sun is radiated back into the atmosphere as **infrared radiation**. Infrared radiation cannot be seen by humans, but we feel it as heat.

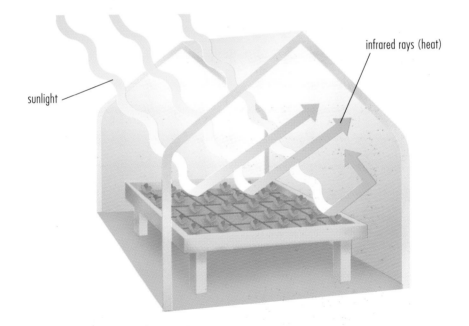

infrared rays (heat)

sunlight

When light enters a greenhouse, the objects inside reflect some of the energy back as heat. The greenhouse glass traps the heat inside the greenhouse. Carbon dioxide, water vapor, and other gases in the atmosphere are called greenhouse gases. They act much like the glass in a greenhouse. Much of the heat radiated by objects on earth cannot escape into space because it is trapped by greenhouse gases. Without the **greenhouse effect**, temperatures on earth would be much lower.

Climate

Every place on earth has its own climate. Climate is the average weather for an area over time. It includes temperature, precipitation, and humidity. Humidity is a measure of the amount of water vapor in the air.

The sun's rays are most direct and strongest at the equator. As you move toward the poles, the sun's rays become more spread out, weaker, and less direct. As a result, the climate at the poles is much colder than the climate at the equator.

Polar climates are cold. The polar regions are close to the North and South Poles. These regions receive precipitation in the form of snow and ice. In some polar areas, the temperature never rises above freezing.

Temperate climates have changing seasons. Temperate regions are between the polar and tropical regions. Winters are usually cold and summers are hot. Some temperate regions receive large amounts of rain and snow. Others receive little.

Tropical climates are warm and moist. The tropical regions are close to the equator. Most tropical regions have steady temperatures with rainfall every day. Others have a rainy wet season and a cooler dry season each year.

Water Cycle

Ninety-seven percent of the water on earth is found in the oceans. The other three percent is freshwater. Most of earth's freshwater is frozen in the polar ice caps and glaciers. The rest is found in surface lakes and streams and underground water supplies.

The water on earth is constantly moving from one place to another and changing from liquid to water vapor and back again. These changes are called the **water cycle**.

Step 1
Heat from the sun causes **evaporation**. Water on earth's surface changes from liquid water to gaseous water vapor.

Step 2
Water vapor rises into the atmosphere and cools, causing **condensation**. Water vapor changes back into liquid water or into solid ice.

Step 3
Water returns to earth's surface when it falls as **precipitation**—rain, sleet, snow, and hail.

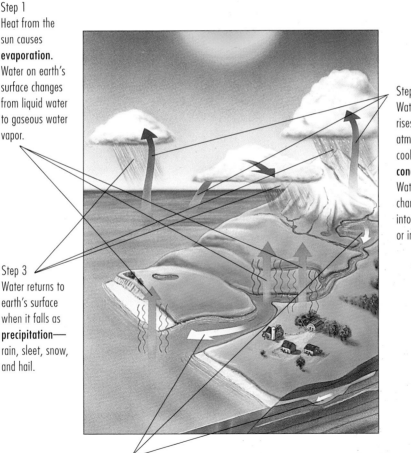

Step 4
On the ground, **runoff** precipitation flows into rivers, lakes, underground reservoirs, and oceans.

Air Rises and Falls

Wind is caused by convection currents in earth's atmosphere. Earth's surface radiates heat. Some parts of the surface radiate more heat than others. The heat is conducted to the air above the surface. (See page 89 for information on heat radiation and conduction.) Air over surfaces that radiate more heat becomes warmer than surrounding air. As the air is warmed, its density decreases and the air rises. When the rising air reaches the colder temperatures of the upper atmosphere, it cools and begins to fall.

Meanwhile, air from cooler areas moves into the space left by the rising warm air. The cooler air is warmed and also starts to rise. This constant rising and falling creates convection currents in the atmosphere. (See page 92 for information on convection currents in earth's mantle.) This movement of air over the earth's surface is called **wind**.

land   warm air rising   cool air moving in to replace warm   ocean

Land absorbs and gives off heat faster than water. During the day, the air over land often becomes warmer than the air over water. The warm air over land rises. The cooler air from the water moves in to take its place. This movement creates a wind that blows onto the land from the water. At night, the situation is reversed. The wind blows in the opposite direction.

Global Winds

The equator receives more direct sunlight than other parts of the globe (see page 108). Air at the equator is heated more than air at the poles. These temperature differences create winds that blow across large areas of the globe.

Warm air rising from the equator moves toward the poles. At latitudes of about 30 degrees north and 30 degrees south, some of this air cools and begins to sink. This moving air forms the **trade winds.** Trade winds blow toward the equator.

Some of the warm air from the equator continues to move toward the poles as it sinks. The rotation of the earth around its axis makes this air move from east to west. This creates winds called **prevailing westerlies.**

High in the atmosphere are fast, strong winds that blow from west to east. The **jet streams** move high above trade winds and prevailing westerlies. The size, location, and strength of jet streams change with the seasons.

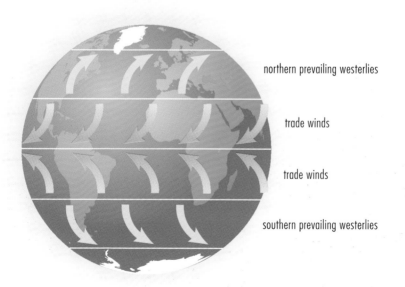

northern prevailing westerlies

trade winds

trade winds

southern prevailing westerlies

Air Masses

Huge bodies of air, called **air masses**, form in the lower parts of the atmosphere. Warm, moist air masses form over tropical regions near the equator. Cold, dry air masses form near the poles. These air masses move, but they do not mix. The movement of air masses causes changes in the weather.

A **front** forms where two air masses with different temperature and humidity come together. A front changes the weather. **Cold fronts** bring stormy weather. **Warm fronts** bring rain and are often followed by hot, humid weather.

Storms

Storms are caused by sudden changes in temperature, precipitation, wind direction, and wind speed. **Thunderstorms** include heavy rainfall, thunder and lightning, and intense gusts of wind. They take place when a cold front collides with a warm front.

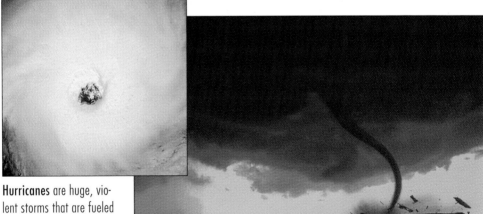

Hurricanes are huge, violent storms that are fueled by warm, moist air in tropical oceans. They lose power as they move over cooler, drier landmasses. They can be hundreds of miles across and last for days or weeks.

Tornadoes are tall, funnel-shaped clouds that twist at very high speeds. They form when cool, dry air collides with warm, moist air. They can be a few hundred feet across and last for a few minutes or a few hours.

The Earth and Beyond

The Moving Earth

Spinning on Its Axis

Earth **rotates**, or spins, around its axis. The **axis** is an imaginary line that runs through the center of the earth, from the north pole to the south pole.

Earth's rotation around its axis creates day and night. It is dark on the side of the planet that is turned away from the sun. It is daylight on the side facing the sun.

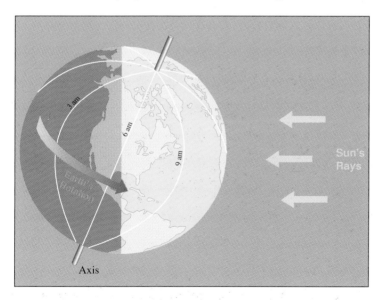

Axis

As the earth spins, the line dividing darkness from light travels over the surface of the planet. To observers on earth, the sun appears to rise above the horizon at dawn, then move across the sky. At sunset, the sun appears to drop below the horizon.

Revolving Around the Sun

Earth is also **orbiting**, or revolving, around the sun. Earth travels at a speed of about 30 kilometers per second and takes one year to complete one orbit.

The Reasons for Seasons

Earth's axis is tilted. The combination of this tilt with earth's annual orbit around the sun causes the seasons to change. A **hemisphere** is half of the globe. The hemisphere that is tilted toward the sun receives more direct rays than the hemisphere that is tilted away from the sun. The hemisphere that is tilted toward the sun also has more daylight hours. The combination of direct rays and longer days makes the weather warmer.

Winter changes to spring on the **vernal equinox,** which is usually March 20 or 21 in the Northern Hemisphere. Summer changes to fall on the **autumnal equinox,** which is usually September 22 or 23 in the Northern Hemisphere. **Equinox** means "equal night." At both equinoxes, the number of daylight hours equals the number of nighttime hours.

Spring changes to summer at the **summer solstice**, which usually falls on June 20 or 21 in the Northern Hemisphere. The summer solstice is the longest day of the year. Fall changes to winter at the **winter solstice**, which usually falls on December 21 or 22 in the Northern Hemisphere. The winter solstice is the shortest day of the year.

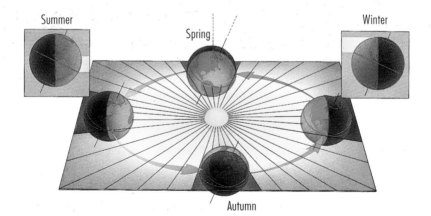

During summer in the Northern Hemisphere, the northern part of the globe is tilted toward the sun. During winter, it is tilted away from the sun. When it is winter in the Northern Hemisphere, it is summer in the Southern Hemisphere.

Earth's Satellite

The moon is about one-quarter the size of earth. Its diameter measures about 3,476 kilometers. The average distance between the earth and the moon is 384,403 kilometers. The moon has about one-sixth the gravity of earth.

The Surface of the Moon

The moon has no atmosphere and no water. The parts of the moon's surface that are in shadow or facing away from the sun are much colder than anyplace on earth. The parts of the moon lit by the sun get very hot.

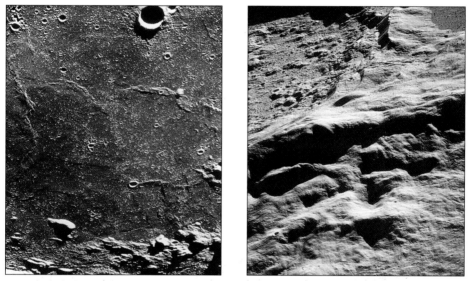

The surface of the moon has mountains thousands of meters high. It also has deep craters that were formed by the impact of meteors. The moon's smooth plains appear as dark areas when seen through a telescope on earth. These lowlands are called **maria**.

Movements of the Moon

The moon revolves around the earth in an elliptical orbit. An **ellipse** is a flattened, or oblong, circle. The moon also rotates on its axis as it revolves around the earth. It takes the moon 27.3 days to turn once on its axis. It also takes the moon 27.3 days to orbit the earth. As a result, the same side of the moon is always facing earth. The opposite side of the moon is never visible from earth.

Phases of the Moon

The 27.3 days it takes for the moon to complete one earth orbit is called a **lunar month**. To an observer on earth, the appearance of the moon changes as it moves through the lunar month. These changes have to do with how the moon and the earth change positions relative to the sun. The changing shapes of the moon are known as the **phases** of the moon.

The moon is bright because it reflects the light of the sun. The positions of the moon and earth relative to the sun change as the moon orbits the earth. This movement changes the way sunlight reflects off the moon.

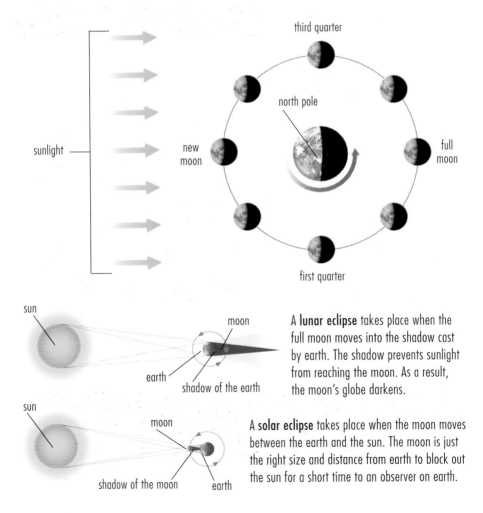

A **lunar eclipse** takes place when the full moon moves into the shadow cast by earth. The shadow prevents sunlight from reaching the moon. As a result, the moon's globe darkens.

A **solar eclipse** takes place when the moon moves between the earth and the sun. The moon is just the right size and distance from earth to block out the sun for a short time to an observer on earth.

The Planets of the Solar System

Nine planets orbit our sun. The inner planets are Mercury, Venus, Earth, and Mars. They are small and rocky. The outer planets are Jupiter, Saturn, Uranus, Neptune, and Pluto. Except for Pluto, the outer planets are huge and made of gas. Pluto is small and rocky.

Planet	Diameter	Average distance from sun	Year length	Composition of atmosphere	Surface	Temperature
Mercury	4,889 km	56 million km	88 Earth days	Helium and hydrogen	Rocky	427° C to -168° C
Venus	12,131 km	108 million km	225 Earth days	Carbon dioxide and nitrogen	Rocky	463° C
Earth	12,784 km	150 million km	365 Earth days	Nitrogen and oxygen	Rocky	16° C
Mars	6,802 km	227 million km	1.88 Earth years	Carbon dioxide, nitrogen, and argon	Rocky	26° C to -123° C
Jupiter	143,306 km	779 million km	12 Earth years	Hydrogen and helium	Liquid hydrogen	-117° C
Saturn	120,808 km	1.4 billion km	29 Earth years	Hydrogen and helium	Liquid hydrogen	-179° C
Uranus	51,233 km	2.9 billion km	84 Earth years	Hydrogen, helium, and methane	Hydrogen, helium, and methane	-171° C
Neptune	49,640 km	4.5 billion km	165 Earth years	Hydrogen, helium, and methane	Liquid water, ammonia, and methane	-207° C
Pluto	2,305 km	5.8 billion km	248 Earth years	Methane and nitrogen	Frozen water and methane	-229° C

Pluto   Neptune   Uranus   Saturn   Jupiter   Mars   Earth   Venus   Mercury   Sun

The Sun–Our Own Star

At the center of the solar system, about 150 million kilometers from earth, is a medium-sized star we call the sun. Placed end to end, about 109 earths could fit across its diameter. If the sun were hollow, a million earths could fit inside. The sun is about 4.6 billion years old, and it is similar to many other stars.

The sun is a giant nuclear furnace. Inside its **core**, hydrogen and helium undergo nuclear fusion reactions and produce massive amounts of energy, including heat, light, and other forms of radiation. Surrounding the core is the sun's atmosphere, which can be divided into three layers. The innermost layer of the sun's atmosphere is the **photosphere**. It can be seen in photographs as the yellow globe of the sun. Gases from the **chromosphere** may stream thousands of kilometers into space. The **corona** can be seen when the moon blocks the light of the photosphere during a solar eclipse, or it can be viewed with special equipment.

Sunspots are cool, dark regions that appear in the photosphere. The location and number of sunspots changes over days and months. **Solar flares** are bright flashes of light that sometimes form near sunspots. Solar flares send enormous amounts of energy into space. Sunspots and solar flares disturb radio and television communications on earth.

Comets, Asteroids, and Meteors

The sun and the planets are not the only objects found in the solar system.

Comets are chunks of ice, dust, rock, and frozen gas. Comets originate outside the solar system, but they are pulled in by the sun's gravity. As a comet nears the sun, a cloud of dust and gas called a **coma** forms around it. Part of this cloud streams out from the comet to form its **tail**.

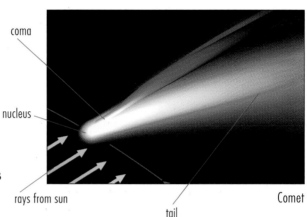

coma

nucleus

rays from sun

tail

Comet

Asteroids are chunks of rock orbiting the sun. Most asteroids are found in an asteroid belt between the orbits of Mars and Jupiter.

Meteoroids are small pieces of matter floating in space. They may be as small as dust grains or as large as boulders. When a meteoroid enters earth's atmosphere, it becomes a **meteor**. Friction with the atmosphere makes meteors glow as they streak across the sky, and people sometimes call them shooting stars. Most meteors burn up completely before they reach the ground. A meteor that falls to the surface of the earth is a **meteorite**.

The Galaxy and Beyond

Stars

Stars are glowing spheres of hot gases. Inside the sun and other stars, nuclear fusion reactions change hydrogen into helium. Stars form inside huge clouds of dust and gas called **nebulae**. Once a star is born, it changes over time. Most stars burn for billions of years.

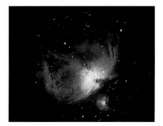

Gravity can pull the material in a nebula together to form a star.

Brightness of Stars

Some stars appear bright in the sky, while others appear dim. Many stars are so dim they cannot be seen without the help of a telescope. Many more cannot be seen from earth at all.

The farther away the star is, the dimmer its light will seem. A bright star that is far away can appear much less bright than a dim star that is nearby. The brightness of a star also depends on its size. Giant and supergiant stars can be 10 to 1,000 times larger than the sun. White dwarf stars can be smaller than earth.

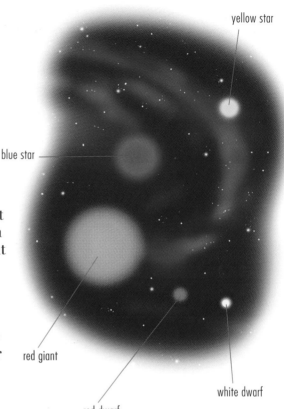

yellow star

blue star

red giant

white dwarf

red dwarf

The color and brightness of a star depend on its temperature. The hottest stars are blue. The coolest stars glow with a red light. Yellow stars, like the sun, are medium in temperature. Types of stars have names based on their colors.

Constellations—Patterns in the Sky

The Big Dipper constellation has bright stars and a shape that is easy to recognize.

Constellations are groups of stars you can see with the naked eye. The constellations were named by ancient Greeks and Romans who imagined seeing characters from myths and legends outlined by the stars. Today, the constellations are best seen away from city lights, on a clear night.

Galaxies

Stars are not spread out evenly through the universe. They are grouped together in **galaxies**. Galaxies also contain clouds of gas and dust.

Spiral galaxy

Our solar system is located in a spiral-shaped galaxy known as the **Milky Way**. Our galaxy contains about 200 billion stars. The stars of the Milky Way revolve around the center of the galaxy. The sun makes one complete orbit every 240 million years.

Elliptical galaxy

Not all galaxies are shaped like spirals. Elliptical galaxies have an oval shape. Irregular galaxies have no particular shape.

Measuring Distances in Space

The universe is so large it cannot be measured in miles or kilometers. Astronomers use special units to measure the vast distances of outer space.

Irregular galaxy

Light travels faster than anything else in the universe. In a year, light travels almost 10 trillion kilometers (10,000,000,000,000 kilometers). The distance light travels in one year is called a **light year.** Scientists measure distances between stars in light years.

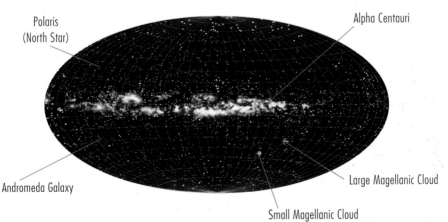

Polaris (North Star)

Alpha Centauri

Andromeda Galaxy

Large Magellanic Cloud

Small Magellanic Cloud

The Milky Way as seen from earth.

Studying the Universe

Humans have traveled to the moon and orbited earth aboard spacecraft and the space shuttle. But space is so vast that sending astronauts to more distant destinations is not practical. Scientists have developed a number of tools and technologies for exploring the sun, the planets, and outer space.

Telescopes

Telescopes were the first instruments humans used to explore the stars and planets. **Optical telescopes** are used to view the visible light given off by distant objects. Other types of telescopes gather information about radio waves, X rays, ultraviolet light, and other forms of radiation given off by astronomical objects.

Scientists can combine the information from many radio telescopes arranged over a large area so that they act like one giant receiver.

The Hubble Space Telescope orbits earth as an artificial satellite. It provides a clear view of objects that cannot be seen through telescopes on earth.

Space Probes

Space probes are robot devices sent out into the solar system to gather information about the planets and the sun. Probes broadcast data back to astronomers on earth. The National Aeronautics and Space Administration (NASA) has launched many probes to explore the solar system.

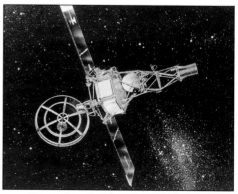

Mariner 2 studied Venus's atmosphere in 1962.

Index